MEDIEVAL
CROSS STITCH
SAMPLERS

1

MEDIEVAL
CROSS STITCH
SAMPLERS

Historical Background

This volume brings to the attention of cross-stitchers some of the wonderful wealth of source material available from the decorative arts of the medieval period and gives examples of how such work can provide inspiration for your own design work, paying particular attention to the stained glass, illuminated manuscripts, heraldry and tapestry of the era.

Restlessness, experimentation and a determined quest for knowledge, in both the artistic and scientific worlds, were the underlying forces during the period we term the Middle or Medieval Age. An exciting time, when the classical ideal of achieving a sense of permanence through the balance between art and nature was re-examined and rejected. The flowering of new intellectual thought prompted the creation of the first great universities of Paris, Oxford and Cambridge. Experimentation with new architectural styles produced lighter and taller buildings, culminating in the new French Gothic style of cathedral and church buildings, such as at Paris and Laon, and the flowering of the Early English adaptation, as found in Salisbury's cathedral.

Let us look at the four crafts I have chosen to concentrate on in their historical context.

To affect the new design in cathedral building, larger windows were required and these then needed to be filled with some form of decoration. The glass painter's craft had always been held in high esteem due in large part, aside from the obvious skill factor, to the high cost of the materials involved. Glass was precious and re-cycling was common; many examples throughout Europe can be found of this thriftiness.

Glass for the windows was produced by a general glassmaker, who also made items for domestic use. He was paid twice as much for coloured glass as for plain, it being bought by merchants by weight, not size. Metallic oxides were added to the molten glass to give the vibrant colouring. 'Ruby' or red glass had an additional process. In its simple form the intensity of colour was so dark it allowed very little light to travel through. To solve this problem, the makers developed the technique of 'flashing', which involved taking clear glass, dipping it into molten red, then working the two together to produce a laminate. This technique was extended to include other colours in the later Middle Ages, as the artist realised its potential in design, particularly for adding detail by scratching or abrading the 'flashed' glass to reveal the colour below.

Subject wise, the 13th century window became highly narrative and naturally more figures featured in the panels. As the design of the window shape became wider and deeper, these figures were often surrounded by geometric shapes and/or intricate, foliage-based borders. Also during this period, as an alternative to or in conjunction with the panels, the 'rose' window found its place. It quickly developed in all its splendour, often to monumental proportions, with an ever-increasing complexity of design. Because of its size, complete stories, usually from the Bible, could be depicted in great detail.

Grisaille glass panels also found prominence during the 13th century.

◆ A beautiful piece of 15th century stained glass in Bourges Cathedral, France.

'Grisailling' describes the dense line work and cross-hatching used to decorate predominately clear glass in buildings where greater light was required, e.g. cloisters and chapter houses. The 'Five Sisters' series of panels in York Minster, England, is a superb example of this technique.

During the latter part of the medieval period as stained glass design continued to evolve, the dense, colour-packed windows of the 13th century were replaced by more white glass, heavily grisailled and by elongated figures with overhead canopies, which were ever more intricately ornamented. The window designs became more sympathetic to the window shape and the content more naturalistic. Colour tones softened: red and blue glass were used less and more nature-based hues of green and brown predominated. The heavily coloured, richer designs were still produced, however.

Together with this greater naturalism, scenes within scenes and heraldic devices began to feature, usually due to the patron or commissioner of the windows insisting that credit be given to his part in the window-making process. More and more of these patrons came from the secular section of society and included both individuals and the newly formed guilds. Such people now looked to embellish their

◆ **'Flower's Ordinary' of c.1520. The ordinary is a pictorial dictionary showing different treatments of checked banners and shields.**

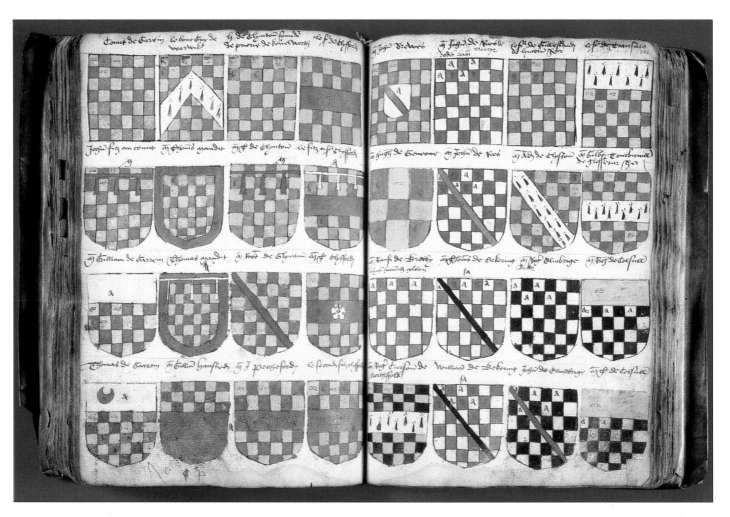

own homes with stained glass panels, which often would contain family armorial crests.

Heraldic seals first appeared in Europe in the second half of the 12th century and provided in their simple geometric designs the first evidence of heraldry. Families, countries and cities, proud of their place in society wished to lay claim to and display their importance and needed a way to demonstrate this. What better way than pictorially through distinctive personal emblems? These also had the practical uses of marking possession and providing a rallying point in battle. The emblems soon became hereditary as they were passed from one generation to the next within a family. As well as providing a good historical account through the ages, heraldry has given us a new and dramatic art form. Certain rules concerning the use of colour and detailing existed from the start and continue to be effective today; these are discussed in their simplest form later in the book (see page 33).

Pen and colour also found form within the beautiful illuminated manuscripts of this age. During the early period most work of this nature was undertaken by monks, when monasteries were the main seats of learning and therefore the chief customers for books. Some monasteries actually earned a profitable income from the production of religious books for churches and other newly formed monasteries. Providing education for the sons of wealthy landowners and merchants, for whom books were needed, also generated business.

During the first half of the 12th century the lower Rhineland and Meuse valley became particularly famous for its gold and enamel work and its influence on illumination eventually spread throughout Europe. Towards the close of the 12th century large lectern books were produced by teams of scribes and illustrators and so, too, were herbal remedy books for private use: the first self-help manuals, as the illustrations would aid the reader in not making a mistake when concocting the remedies. Unfortunately, over a period of time these remedy books became highly stylised as illustrators took copies from previously written books rather than directly from the plants.

With the inauguration in the 13th century of the first universities, the monastic monopoly on centres of learning was broken and many more secular scribes and illustrators were to be found often living amongst the other craftsmen in towns and villages, plying their trade through commission. The work of the monasteries, however, did not cease. The upkeep of large religious houses must have been enormous and book making and illustration helped balance the books! Liturgical manuscripts, psalters (personal prayer books which also contained a calendar of saints days) and Books of Hours (religious and secular stories as an aid to private worship) were produced. As more of the populace became educated, the demand for books also grew and soon histories were being translated from Latin into French, a language spoken universally by the upper strata of society.

The 14th century brought a better quality of botanical illustration into the manuscripts. Books of all sizes and subjects were now in demand, ranging from small, beautifully illustrated, personal bibles through large format volumes of liturgical music, suitable to be seen by many people at once, to stories of romance and history.

Gutenberg's printing press invented in the middle of the 15th century did not have an immediate adverse effect on the demand for manuscripts. Because of its scarcity, it was just as easy to order a book written by hand as it was a printed one.

Another area of great skill and design that flourished at this time was needlework. Most of the embroidery which survives is ecclesiastical, though secular embroidery and design can be researched by viewing the contemporary paintings, manuscripts and tapestries.

By the 11th century the dyeing and weaving of wool, linen and silk had reached a very high standard; wool and linen particularly in Europe, silk in Italy and the East. Silk thread was used highly skilfully in embroidery on all heraldic work and to embellish the domestic garments of the wealthy. English ecclesiastical embroidery, in particular during the 13th and 14th centuries, gained great repute. Many copes, mitres and maniples are still in existence and involve much silk thread work. The stitching was carried out by women of all social classes and it was considered absolutely imperative to be proficient at such skills.

Historical panels are also evident, the most widely known of which, The Bayeux Tapestry, was worked in laid and couched stitching of wool on linen.

Quilting and whitework were undertaken, for practical reasons as well as aesthetic. The first grew from the need to thicken and pad cloth to aid its heat retention properties and the second was used on articles which would require frequent laundering and on which, therefore, coloured threads might well fade.

The tapestry work of the period produced some truly beautiful

◆ A detail from a 15th century French Book of Hours showing the complexity of manuscript illumination, which encompassed religious painting and botanical illustration as well as fine calligraphy.

designs, particularly in the 14th and 15th centuries. We are lucky that quite a few examples are still in existence; greatly treasured by the museums or great houses that hold them. The oldest example of the 'verdure' style (in which plants feature strongly) is the armorial panel of Philip the Good, created in 1466 by Jean Le Haze and now held in the Historical Museum in Berne, Switzerland. Verdure or 'mille fleurs' (literally, 'a thousand flowers') tapestries were usually woven in wool and silk to a pre-drawn pattern. Backgrounds were sometimes worked in green in later years but were predominantly of red, white or yellow.

There were three principal stages in tapestry production. First, the artist would design small scale 'models' of the compositions. The cartoonist would then transpose the design, using the

◆ A close-up of the spectacular abundance of flowers woven into the background of 'The Lady and the Unicorn': a medieval French tapestry.

'models', to the required full size. Finally, the weavers reproduced the cartoons, using their own weaving techniques. With so many creative people involved, it is understandable that tempers sometimes became a little frayed! On one occasion, in 1476, a law suit was brought, the outcome of which (but to apply only around the Brussels region) was to allow cartoonists and weavers free licence only with the delineation of foliage and animals, leaving the rest to the painters, who had felt their art was becoming distorted by the craftsmen.

It was first thought that these tapestries were worked by groups of craftsmen, who moved from place to place executing the commission on site. Lately, information has come to light which disputes this and it is now thought that centres of tapestry production grew up around the Burgundian Netherlands, Brussels, Ghent, Arras, Lille and Tournai. The craftsmen of one workshop would often be sub-contracted to another and this is one of the main reasons for the difficulty there often is in defining precisely a tapestry's workshop origin, unless there is contemporary written evidence.

A general glossary, then, of some aspects of the medieval wealth of decorative arts. It is, of course, by no means comprehensive, limited space will not allow, but hopefully the information included will be of interest to you as you now set to work!

Floral Commemorative Sampler

The flower designs for this sampler are taken from the exquisite tapestry, 'The Lady and the Unicorn', which now hangs in the Cluny Museum in Paris. Many armorial tapestries were woven in the medieval period and so, too, tapestries in the 'mille fleurs' style. 'Armorial' relates to the use of heraldic devices within the tapestry, either denoting who commissioned the work, or in honour of some particular person. The term 'mille fleurs' refers to the style of covering both the background and the foreground with densely-strewn foliage and plants, using the commonly-found flowers, trees and leaves of the country of origin of the tapestry. The 'Lady' is, in fact, the finest example of the merging of these two styles, and why I choose it when deciding which of the medieval weavings to base design work upon.

'The Lady' is a series of six panels woven between the years 1484-1500. All the panels are worked on a red background with a dark blue central island, on which the Lady stands, surrounded by birds, beasts and trees and usually accompanied by a lady-in-waiting.

◆ **Left: The panel from 'The Lady and the Unicorn' tapestry depicting 'Touch'. Right: Some of the abundant flowers from the medieval tapestry decorate this sampler for a specially happy occasion.**

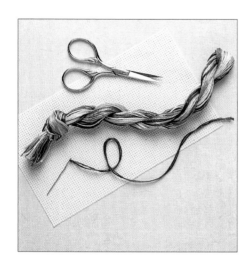

Each of the first five panels is concerned in its theme with one of the five senses and shows the Lady involved in an illustrative activity. The flowers decorating the red background are suspended flowering branches, which is symbolic of the custom of strewing flowers on feast or fête days, while the flowers on the blue island are actually growing out of the ground. The tapestry is further embellished with decorated standards, escutcheons and banners; a horn and a unicorn giving it a mystical aura.

The final panel in the series has continued to puzzle scholars as to its meaning. Many theories have been proffered. The inscription on the tent in this panel reads, "A mon seul désir" (to my only desire), while the lady is seen with a necklace in her hand. On first view it seems she is lifting the piece from a jewellery box, but she is, in fact, replacing it, laying it aside, and thus the words can be understood in this context as meaning the putting aside of possessions which might cause undesirable emotions and behaviour. If this is so, then the panels portray a very strong moral message!

Discovered in an unrenovated state by the writer, George Sand, in 1844, at a château in Boussac, France, it was eventually acquired by the Cluny Museum 39 years later and renovated.

Many suggestions have been made as to its origin and history, many romantic in notion but with little historical evidence. The most likely clue is in the arms of the Le Viste family, which are featured on the work. The Le Viste family found prominence in the service of King Louis XI and it is highly probable that Jean Le Viste commissioned the work as a proclamation of his increased status and wealth.

As to the identification of the work's designer or painter, even less information has been unearthed. From its style it is obviously French, though confusingly the style of the lady's clothing is essentially Italian. As to where it was made, one can only speculate. The 'mille fleurs' backgrounds of the panels show flora from Northern Europe, so they may have been woven at the Loire workshops or in Brussels.

If you are ever fortunate enough to visit Paris, please do make time to visit the Cluny Museum and view this exquisite work, so dramatically displayed in its own specially constructed, circular and darkened room. In the meantime, either in memory or in anticipation of such a delight, I have taken some of the woven flowers from three of the panels and recreated them in cross stitch.

This design shows aquilegias, violas and yellow daisies grouped to form the border for a sampler, which could commemorate a family event, such as a wedding anniversary or the birth of a child. I have tried to keep the colours close to those of the original tapestry, although the forms vary slightly to aesthetically compliment each other and the overall balance of the design. Each of the motifs can also be used separately as shown on the mirror and hairbrush of the dressing table set or interlaced as shown on the clothes brush project which follows.

METHOD

As this is quite a detailed project which will take some time to complete, I strongly recommend that you hem or tack the raw edges of the fabric before starting to cross stitch, in order to prevent fraying (see page 90).

Measure 4 in (10 cm) up from the bottom right corner of the fabric and 4 in (10 cm) in from the righthand side and begin work at this point, following the starting stitch marked on the chart on page 21.

Use two strands of cotton, working over one thread intersection. Work the flowers and leaves in cross stitch and the outlines and stems in back stitch.

Stitch the lower horizontal line of the border first, then work the lower lefthand flower motif. Continue with the left vertical border, then work the upper lefthand flowers. Next stitch the right vertical border, followed by the flower motif and enclose by working the top right hand border.

When the stitching is completed, wash if necessary and press gently from the wrong side (see page 90).

For finishing and mounting instructions, see page 92.

MATERIALS

1 piece of cream Aida, 16 count, 19 x 17 in (48.5 x 43 cm)

tapestry needle, size 26

lightweight wadding for mounting (optional)

1 skein each of stranded cotton in the following shades:

		DMC	Anchor
border and lettering			
	dusky pink	316	969
aquilegias			
	mauve	210	108
	pink	605	50
	blue	517	170
	green	989	242
	dark green	501	878
	dark peach	352	9
	blue green	562	210
	peach	353	6
	yellow	3078	292

back stitch stems
  greens as above

violas

		DMC	Anchor
	blue	798	131
	light blue	809	130
	dark blue	517	170
	grey	413	401
	brown/yellow	676	891
	red	817	19

  greens as above
back stitch stems
  blue green as above
back stitch flowers
  grey as above

daisies
  greens as above

		DMC	Anchor
	brown	3064	883
	yellow	726	295

back stitch stems
  green and blue green as above

Finished size of design: 11 x 9 in (28 x 23 cm)

◆ **Left: A detail from the 'Taste' panel of 'The Lady and the Unicorn' tapestry.**

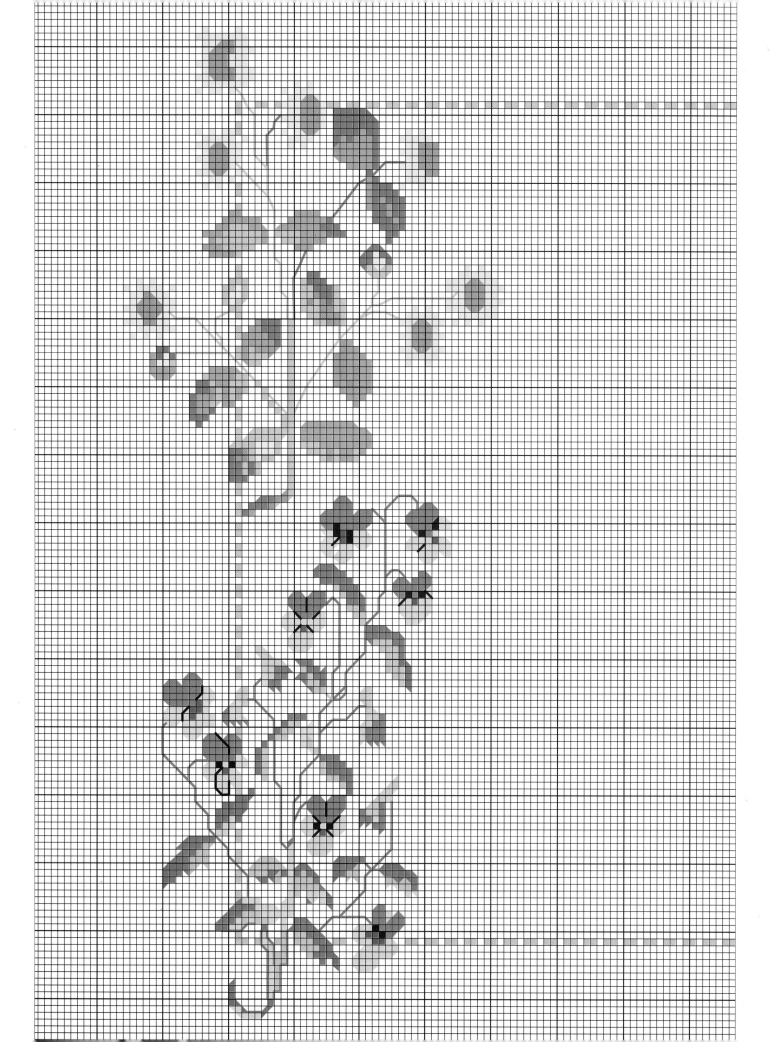

Extend here if
more space needed
for larger name

Extend here if
more space needed
for larger name

Dressing Table Set

The three projects which make up this delicate dressing table set all use some of the same flower motifs from 'The Lady and the Unicorn' tapestry as have been used on the Commemorative Sampler on page 17. I hope in this way to demonstrate the versatility of the sampler designs. All the same shades of stranded cotton are used, so you should have plenty of leftovers if you have already stitched the sampler.

METHOD

Work as follows for all three pieces.

Fold the Aida in half lengthwise and crosswise to find the centre point. Crease lightly. Start work at this point following the stitch marked on the relevant chart on this or the next page.

Use two strands of cotton over one thread intersection for the mirror and hairbrush designs and one strand of cotton over one intersection for the clothes brush. Work the flowers and leaves in cross stitch and the outlines and stems in back stitch.

When the stitching is completed, wash if necessary and press gently from the wrong side (see page 90). Place the interfacing centrally on the reverse of the work and iron in position. Trim and mount the piece following the manufacturer's instructions.

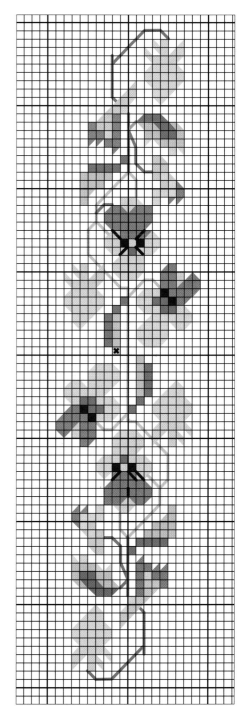

◆ Left: The flower motifs also look good on pieces for the dressing table.
Far left: One of the five panels from 'The Lady and the Unicorn' tapestry depicting the senses: this one shows 'Smell'.

Mirror

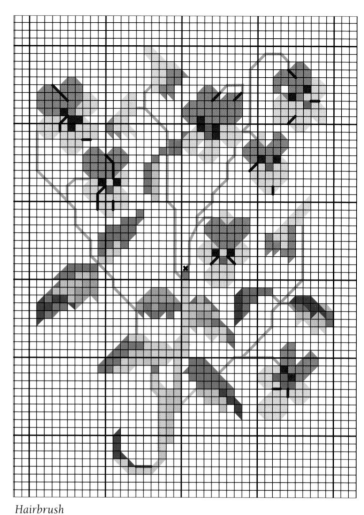

Hairbrush

MATERIALS

1 piece of white Aida, 16 count, 7 x 7 in (18 x 18 cm), for the mirror

1 piece of white Aida, 18 count, 5 x 6 in (12.5 x 15 cm), for the hairbrush

1 piece of white Aida, 22 count, 4 x 8 in (10 x 20 cm), for the clothes brush

tapestry needle, size 26

3 pieces of iron-on interfacing, same size as 3 Aida pieces

1 dressing table blank set (see page 93 for stockists)

1 skein each of stranded cotton in the following shades:

		DMC	Anchor
aquilegias			
	mauve	210	108
	pink	605	50
	blue	517	170
	green	989	242
	dull green	501	878
	blue green	562	210
	dark peach	352	9
	peach	353	6
	yellow	3078	292

back stitch stems
green and blue green as above

violas			
	blue	798	131
	light blue	809	130
	dark blue	517	170
	grey	413	401
	brown/yellow	676	891
	red	817	19

back stitch stems
  dull green as above

back stitch flowers
  grey as above

Finished size of design, mirror: 2 ½ x 3 ⅝ in (6 x 9.5 cm)

Finished size of design, hairbrush: 2 ¼ x 3 in (5.5 x 7.5 cm)

Finished size of design, clothes brush: ⅞ x 3 ⅝ in (2.2 x 9.2 cm)

Crystal Pot

A fusion of flower motifs taken both from 'The Lady and the Unicorn' tapestry and from an exquisite miniature Book of Hours compiled in Tours or Paris around 1470-90(see page 60): this design combines motifs taken from the Commemorative Sampler on page 17 and the Alphabet Sampler on page 50. The vibrancy of the flower colours has not faded with time. Shown in the photograph on page 23 on a crystal pot, the design would also work well in an oval mount as a picture or greetings card. Use threads leftover from the sampler projects if you have already worked them.

METHOD

Fold the Aida in half lengthwise and crosswise to find the centre point. Crease lightly. Start work at this point following the stitch marked on the chart below.

Use two strands of cotton over one thread intersection. Work the flower outlines and stems in back stitch, the rest in cross stitch.

When the stitching is completed, wash if necessary and press gently from the wrong side (see page 90). Place the interfacing centrally on the reverse of the work and iron in position. Trim and mount the piece following the manufacturer's instructions.

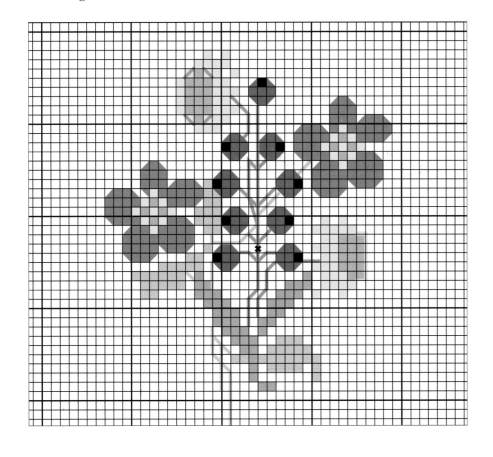

MATERIALS

1 piece of white Aida, 18 count, 4 ½ x 4 ½ in (11.5 x 11.5 cm)

1 piece of iron-on interfacing, same size as Aida

tapestry needle, size 26

1 crystal pot, 4 in (10 cm) diameter lid (see page 93 for stockists)

1 skein each of stranded cotton in the following shades:

		DMC	Anchor
	yellow	727	293
	brown	3064	883
	red	349	13
	black	310	403
	blue	792	177
	blue green	562	210
	green	368	214

Finished size of design: 1 ⅞ x 2 ¼ in (4.8 x 5.5 cm)

Stained Glass Window Sampler

This design, which is also featured on the cover of the book, has two sources of inspiration. The first, for the cross-hatched, lattice work, is a stained-glass Bible window from c. 1280. It was made for a Dominican church in Cologne. In 1804 the church was destroyed but thankfully the glass was rescued and subsequently placed in Cologne Cathedral. The second, for the inset flower, is a detail on the 'Sight' panel of 'The Lady and the Unicorn' tapestry which is described on page 16.

The stained glass artist during the medieval period was often the painter as well as the designer. He would be provided with rough sketches by the funder and it would be his responsibility to bring these into full relief. Paper was scarce and vellum expensive, so the full size pattern would be drawn, with charcoal, onto a table, usually white-washed. Sections of the design would then be catalogued with symbols to define the intended colours. Upon this table, the cutter, painter and assemblers would work to complete the project.

Paper became more available on the continent during the mid to late 14th century and 'cartoons' began to be used instead of the table-technique. The 'cartoon' would be hung in the studio to act as a guide rather than a template, a system which is still in use today.

Once the pattern was drawn, glass was cut roughly to shape using a heated iron, then carefully trimmed; next came the highly skilled job of painting with 'geet' or 'arnement'. This was glass paint made from a mixture of ground glass, iron or copper oxide and gum arabic, bound together with wine, water, urine or vinegar. It was made up into various degrees of thickness to suit the effects required, then applied with brushes or quills and sometimes even fingers! The yellow tones of line and wash used by the painters were produced by using silver nitrate or oxide.

The glass was next fired, then 'leaded-up' by placing the pieces back in the right position on the table and setting grooved strips of lead between them to join one to the other. The lead strips often formed an integral part of the design and were not always merely functional.

The beauty of line, the vividness of the jewel colours, the intricacy of design and thankfully the durability of stained glass, have given us a rich and splendid legacy from which to draw our own inspiration.

◆ Below: The inspiration for the lattice work on the sampler comes from this Bible Window now in Cologne Cathedral, Germany.
Left: This sampler is designed to resemble a stained glass panel as well as featuring a background motif from an actual window.

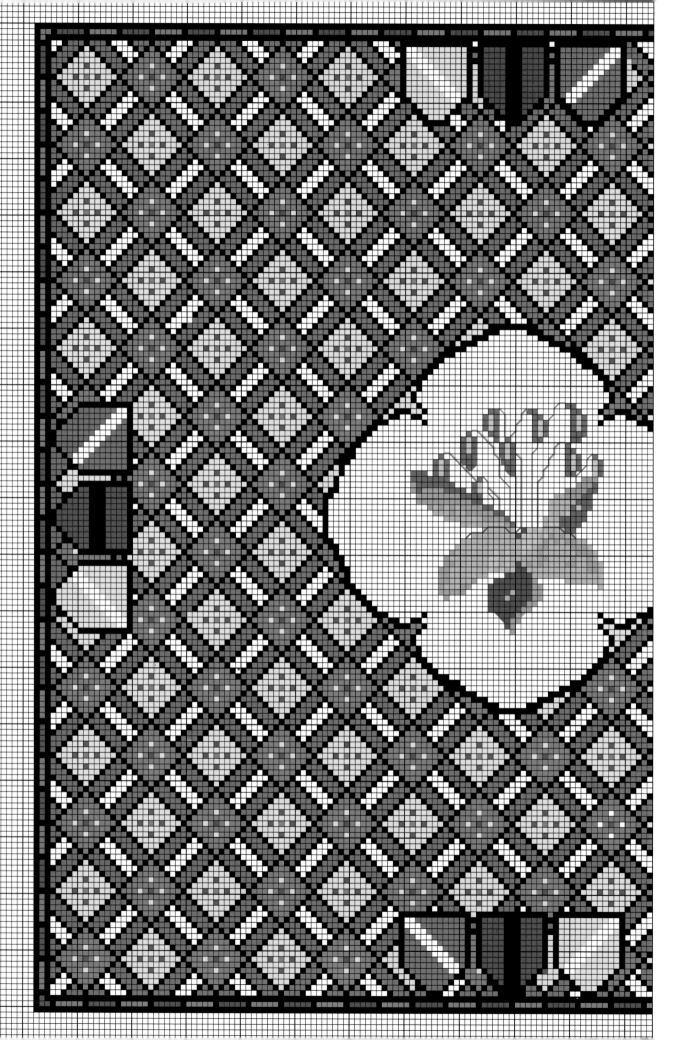

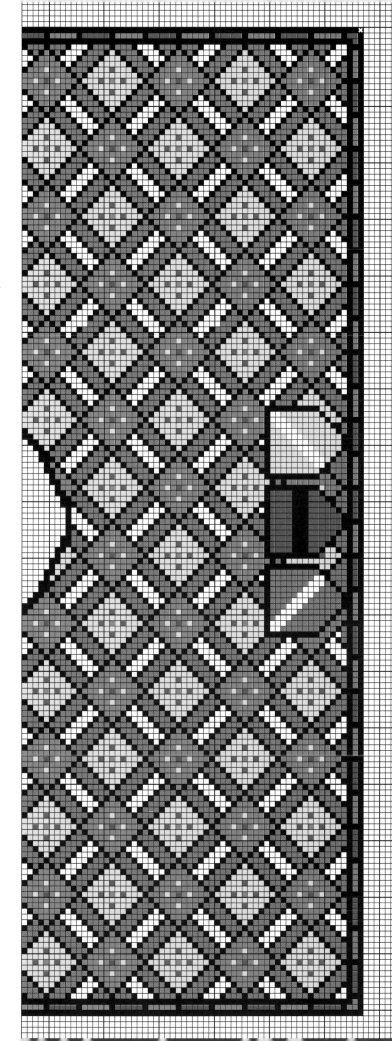

MATERIALS

*1 piece of white Aida, 18 count,
15 ¾ x 15 ¾ in (40 x 40 cm)*

tapestry needle, size 26

lightweight wadding for mounting (optional)

*1 skein each of stranded cotton in the
following shades:*

		DMC	Anchor
■	*black*	310	403
■	*red*	816	44
□	*yellow*	444	291
■	*bright green*	700	228
■	*blue*	798	131
■	*rust*	350	11
□	*gold*	834	874
■	*dark green*	500	879
■	*medium green*	501	878
■	*green*	502	877
□	*pale green*	503	876

*Finished size of design: 9 ¾ x 9 ¾ in
(24.5 x 24.5 cm)*

METHOD

This, like all the samplers, is a detailed project which will take some time to complete, so I recommend that you hem or tack the raw edges of the fabric before starting to cross stitch, to prevent fraying (see page 90).

Measure 3 in (7.5 cm) down from the top right corner of the fabric and 3 in (7.5 cm) in from the righthand side. Begin work at this point following the starting stitch marked on the chart on page 29.

Use two strands of cotton, working over one thread intersection. Work the flower stems in back stitch, the rest in cross stitch. Note that for some of the backstitched flower stems I have used one strand of green and one strand of gold together in the needle for a variegated effect.

I suggest that you stitch the black diagonal lines forming the diamonds first. Working continuous diagonals can be quite fast and will give a framework for the fill-in colours. If you become bored, fill in some of the diamonds or work the central flower motif once the quatrefoil outline has been stitched. Work the four contrast colour stitches in each diamond over the top after stitching all the other fill-in colours.

When the stitching is completed, wash if necessary and press gently from the wrong side (see page 90).

For finishing and mounting instructions, see page 92.

◆ A detail from the 'Sight' panel of
'The Lady and the Unicorn' tapestry.

Spectacles Case

A design based on the lattice work from the Stained Glass Window Sampler inspired by a panel now to be found in Cologne Cathedral. The same shades of cotton have been used, so that you can use up any leftovers from the sampler. Used here to decorate a glasses case, the boldness of the colours should help conquer the 'now-where-did-I-put-my-specs' syndrome!

The design is worked on plastic canvas. If you do not feel inclined to work the lattice pattern all over the reverse side as well, might I suggest you fill the area with one chosen shade inserting just a group of four diamonds centrally. This design has been worked to a standard size. Check the size against your own spectacles and enlarge if necessary.

◆ **The spectacles case needs a good, all-over design for which this lattice work from the Stained Glass Sampler is perfect.**

METHOD

Work the design on both pieces of canvas following the start stitch on the chart on page 32 and leaving two holes on all sides of the canvas free. Work in cross stitch using three strands of cotton over one canvas intersection. When completed assemble the case as follows.

Trim the plastic canvas, leaving only one unworked row of holes all round. Place the two pieces of lining with right sides together and machine stitch or back stitch by hand together round two long and one short sides leaving a ¼ in (6 mm) seam allowance. Turn over a hem around the top opening and slipstitch in position. Lay this lining case onto the reverse side of the back sheet of worked canvas. Using one strand of black, slip stitch the base of the lining to the base of the cover. Now do the same at the top, but of course only catch one side of the lining. Next place the front sheet of the case on the other side of the lining to enclose it and slip stitch the top of the lining and canvas together.

Holding the case together, oversew into the unworked holes using three strands of black all round the three sides, thus binding the back and front together. Finally oversew into the unworked holes around the opening of the case.

31

MATERIALS

*2 pieces of plastic canvas, 14 count mesh,
4 ½ x 7 in (11.5 x 18 cm)*

*2 pieces of lining material ½ in (12 mm)
larger in all directions than canvas*

tapestry needle, size 24

lightweight wadding for mounting (optional)

*1 skein of stranded cotton in the following
shade:*

		DMC	Anchor
▨	red	814	45

2 skeins of stranded cotton in:

▨	yellow	444	291
▨	green	700	228
▨	blue	798	131
▨	black	310	403

*Finished size of design: 4 ⅛ x 6 ½ in
(10.5 x 16.5 cm)*

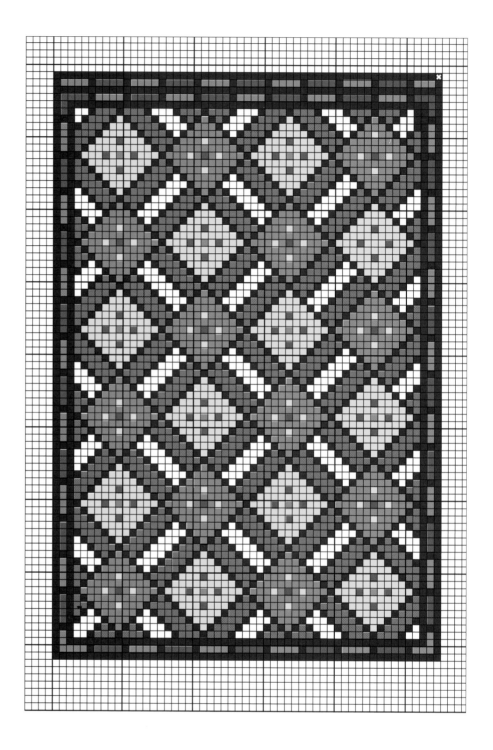

Heraldic Shield Sampler

Sadly, there are very few medieval pennants, flags and other heraldic accoutrements surviving but we do have illuminated manuscripts, rolls of arms and seals that give information on the heraldry of this time.

I have used one such roll as inspiration for this project. The College of Arms' Mowbray's Roll painted c. 1365 shows the bars, bends and crosses of medieval heraldry. Into this I have incorporated an alphabet.

The sampler can be worked exactly as it appears or the outer shield outline could be used as a frame for your own experimentation in drawing, for fun, your own coat of arms. Design motifs or devices to work within the inner shield shapes, then place these within the larger framework and add your family name to personalise it.

To be correct, there are simple rules which should be adhered to. Firstly, any one of the five tinctures or colours used in heraldry must not be placed directly on another, nor one of the two metals upon the other. Metals can be placed on tinctures and vice versa.

Tinctures: red (termed 'gules')
              blue (azure)
              black (sable)
              green (vert)
              purple (purpure)
Metals: gold (or)
              white (argent)

The background colour is called the 'field' and can be a single metal or tincture. It can also be divided or parted. The art of heraldry is a complex one and impossible to cover in these few pages but here in diagram form below and on the right are some of the simple shield designs that may be useful to you with your own designing.

The shields also make a highly decorative emblem for smaller pieces as shown on the bookmark which follows.

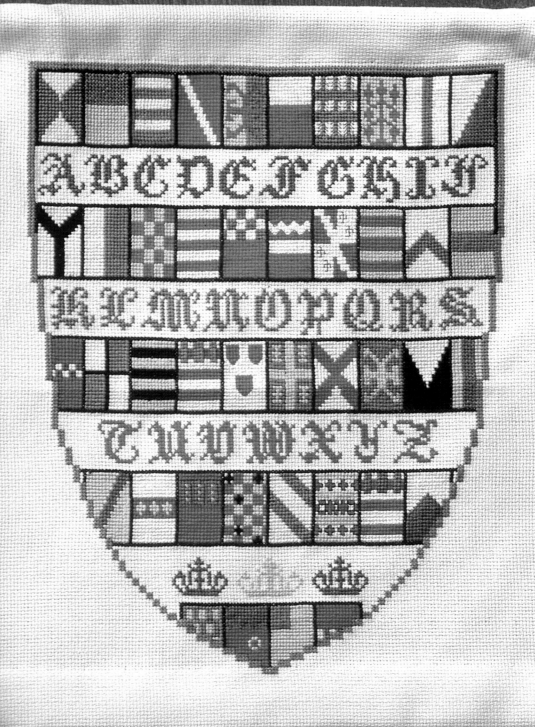

METHOD

This is another detailed project which will take some time to complete, so I recommend that you hem or tack the raw edges of the fabric before starting to cross stitch, to prevent fraying (see page 90).

Measure 3 in (7.5 cm) down from the top right corner of the fabric and 3 in (7.5 cm) in from the righthand side, and begin work at this point following the starting stitch marked on the chart on page 36.

Use three strands of cotton working over one thread intersection. Work any shield detail in backstitch, the rest in cross stitch.

Stitch the horizontal top line of the shield shape. Next work approximately 30 stitches of the right border, then count down to the next black horizontal line and work along for approximately 50 stitches. Now begin to fill in the first row of inner shield designs. Do not stitch the whole outer border at this stage, as you may miscalculate which would affect the positioning of the inner shields: it is much easier to work the outer shape in sections as you complete the inner rows.

After you have completed the first row of shields, work approximately 30 stitches down the left outer border, then commence the first line of letters. Continue in this way, line by line, until complete.

When the stitching is completed, turn back the sides of the piece so that a 1¼ in (4 cm) margin of unworked fabric shows on the right side. Trim the hem allowance to ¾ in (2 cm), turn under the raw edge and slip stitch to secure. Turn back the top and bottom edges to leave the same margin of unworked fabric on the right side, then make a hem large enough to allow the dowel or bell pull ends to be slotted through. Slip stitch in place.

Decorate the hanging with ribbon, braid and tassels as preferred.

MATERIALS

1 piece of white Aida, 14 count, 17 x 19 in (43 x 48.5 cm)

tapestry needle, size 24

1 pair of bell pull ends or 2 lengths of ½ in (1 cm) diameter doweling, 14 in (35.5 cm) long

braid, ribbon or tassels for hanging (optional)

2 skeins each of stranded cotton in the following shades:

		DMC	Anchor
	yellow	725	306
	green	911	230
	red	817	19

3 skeins of stranded cotton in:

		DMC	Anchor
	blue	798	131
	black	310	403
	white	blanc	1
	purple	327	100

Finished size of design: 10¼ x 12¼ in (26 x 31 cm)

◆ Left: This Roll was painted around 1365-70 and shows the simple bars, bends and crosses of early medieval heraldry.
Far left: Shields within a shield provide the decoration for a traditional Alphabet Sampler.

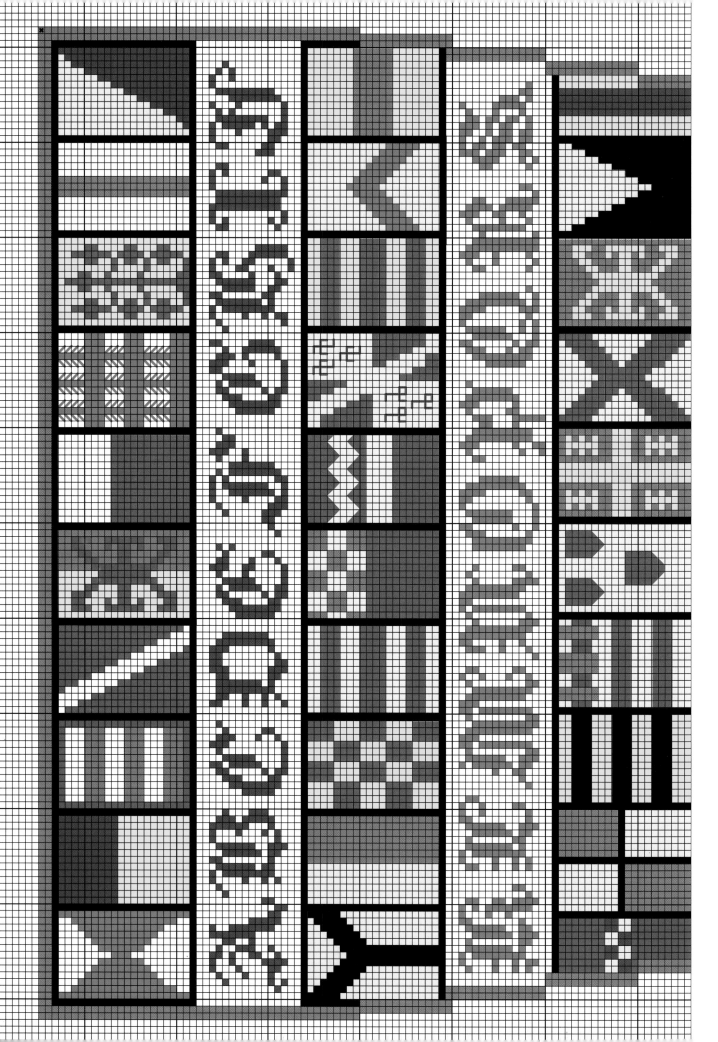

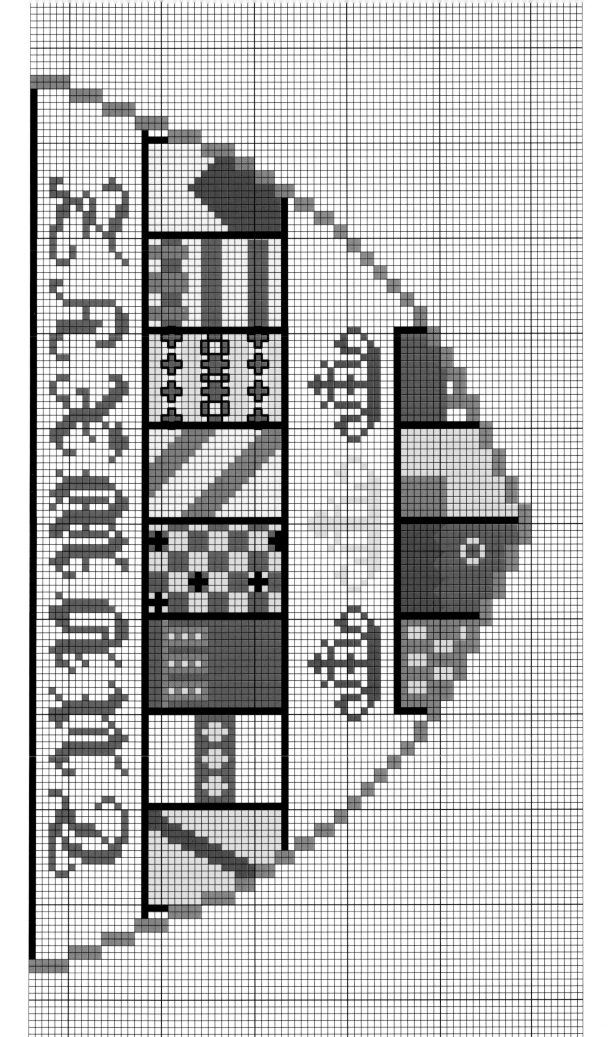

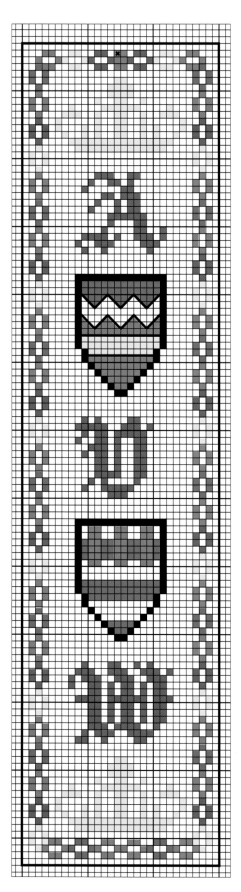

Heraldic Bookmark

This bookmark and the notebooks which follow use some of the motifs from the Heraldic Shield Sampler on page 34 and are included to show possible uses of the sampler chart as a design source. For this bookmark I have worked my own initials between two chosen shields. The chart principally shows the placings on the bookmark of the letters and shields. Any other of the little shields could be used with different letters. You choose!

METHOD

Fold the bookmark in half lengthwise to find the centre vertical line and mark this at the top with a pin. Check the number of threads per inch on the bookmark against the chart on the left. The bookmark counts can vary by one or two squares; if there is a discrepancy, adjust the design accordingly, so that it is centred on the bookmark. Count down the same number of threads on the fabric as there are blank squares on the design chart (allowing for any discrepancy) and begin work with the starting stitch given on the chart.

Use two strands of cotton over one thread intersection. Work any shield detail in backstitch, the rest in cross stitch.

When the stitching is completed, wash if necessary and press gently from the wrong side (see page 90).

Three Notebooks

Three small designs, two showing further usage of the heraldic motifs from the sampler on page 34 and the other a little violet from a diaper design (see page 44). I have included these in the book to demonstrate how easy it is to isolate parts of larger designs to obtain motifs that can form complete projects in their own right. Take time to look through the designs in this book and think how you could apply them or a part of them to other projects and you will find there is a wealth of material.

METHOD

Work as follows for each design.

Fold one of the pieces of Aida in half lengthwise and crosswise to find the centre point. Crease lightly. Start work at this point following the stitch marked on the relevant chart below.

Use three strands of cotton, working over one thread intersection. Work the flower stems in backstitch, the rest in cross stitch.

When the stitching is completed, press lightly from the wrong side, then trim the fabric to just a little smaller than the notebook size.

Peel the sticky plastic from its backing and place centrally on the front of the design. Press in place. Touch a little glue round the edge of the cut-out on the blank and affix the design centrally. Enclose the design by touching the backing sheet edges with glue and joining it to the reverse of the work. Touch a little more glue to the lip of the cover and press in place.

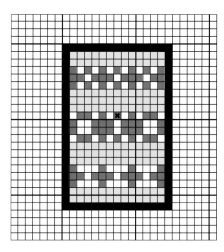

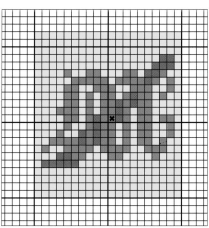

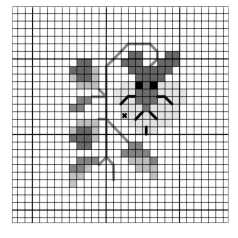

MATERIALS

(Notebooks)

3 notebook mounts (see page 93 for stockists)
fabric adhesive
tapestry needle, size 26 or 24
3 pieces of white Aida, 14 count, 4 x 3 in
(10 x 7.5 cm)
1 skein each of stranded cotton in the
following shades:

		DMC	Anchor
viola design			
	gold	726	295
	dark grey	413	401
	maroon	814	45
	green	989	242
	dull green	501	878
	purple	550	101
initial design			
	yellow	444	291
	bright green	700	228
	purple	550	101
stripes design			
	black	310	403
	maroon	814	45
	yellow	444	291

Finished size of design (all three):
1 1/8 x 1 3/5 in (2.8 x 4 cm)

MATERIALS

(Bookmark)

1 lacy bookmark (see page 93 for stockists)
tapestry needle, size 26
1 skein each of stranded cotton in the
following shades:

		DMC	Anchor
	yellow	725	306
	blue	798	131
	purple	327	100
	red	817	19
	green	911	230
	black	310	403

Finished size of design: 1 1/2 x 6 1/2 in
(4 x 16.5 cm)

◆ **Left: A personalised bookmark and**
| **three notebook designs make good**
| **use of the shield and flower motifs.**

◆ **Above: Details from a medieval illuminated manuscript.**
Right: The traditional band sampler format is used here to display a wide selection of decorative designs from medieval manuscripts.

Band Sampler

The amazing wealth of source material from the Middle Ages and the confines of one volume have prompted this project.

I have organised the patterns in the later, popular style of the 'band' samplers. These were long pieces of fabric on which needlewomen would keep an inventory of worked samples of patterns and stitches, placing their new-found pattern in either horizontal bands or blocks. And in the best tradition of the band sampler, you can take any of the border patterns and use them for other designs, for example on bookmarks or cake bands. Some possibilities are shown in the three following projects on pages 45-8.

Here then is our medieval band sampler, or, strictly speaking, 'pattern book', since the only stitches we are using are cross and back stitch.

The patterns are taken from the following sources, some of which are shown on this and the following pages:

Nos 1 and 4: 11th century manuscripts;
No 2: detail from the Florette Bible; the Transfiguration c. 1156;
Nos 3 and 5: border detail from 12th century manuscript;
Nos 6 and 8: detail from 13th century diapers (see page 66);
Nos 7 and 10: border details from 13th century illuminated manuscripts;
No 9: border detail from 14th century manuscript.

The upper lefthand area is for you to personalise should you so wish, with names and/or dates, or a piece of verse of your choice, using the letters from the Heraldic Shield Sampler on page 34. Alternatively, perhaps you would like to choose another motif from the other design charts in the book. I have signed and dated this sampler along the base. The project could be mounted either as a picture or a wall hanging.

Decorate the hanging with ribbon, braid and tassels as preferred.

◆ Some of the many highly decorative motifs to be found in medieval manuscripts.

MATERIALS

1 piece of cream Belfast linen, 32 count, 15 x 22 in (38 x 56 cm)

or 1 piece of cream Aida, 16 count, same size as linen

tapestry needle, size 24 or 26

lightweight wadding for mounting (optional)

2 lengths of ½ in (1 cm) diameter doweling, each 13 in (33 cm) long (wall hanging only)

ribbon or braid, 18 in (45 cm) in length (wall hanging only)

1 skein each of stranded cotton in the following shades:

		DMC	Anchor
	maroon	315	897
	red	3721	896
	green	367	216
	grey	413	401
	pink	605	335
	blue	793	176
	light blue	809	130
	gold	832	907
	aqua	993	186
	pink	3727	969
	gold metallic		

2 skeins of stranded cotton in:

	lavender	209	109
	light green	563	208
	light gold	834	874

Finished size of design: 8¾ x 15¾ in (22 x 39.5 cm)

METHOD

Measure 3 in (7.5 cm) down from the top right corner of the fabric and 3 in (7.5 cm) in from the righthand side and begin work at this point following the starting stitch marked on the chart on page 42.

Use two strands of cotton, working over two thread intersections if using the Belfast linen and over one thread intersection if using the Aida. Work the outlines in backstitch, the rest in cross stitch.

Work the horizontal border line first, then the appropriate number of vertical stitches to outline the first band design. Now stitch this. Continue in this way until all the bands have been stitched.

The lefthand rectangle has been left for you to personalise your work. Instructions for positioning the letters are given on page 92.

When the stitching is completed, wash if necessary and press gently from the wrong side (see page 90).

To mount the sampler in a frame follow the instructions on page 92. If you wish to display your work as a wall hanging, turn back the sides of the piece so that a 1 in (2.5 cm) margin of unworked fabric shows on the right side. Trim the hem allowance to ¾ in (2 cm), turn under the raw edge and slip stitch to secure. Turn back the top and bottom edges to leave the same margin of unworked fabric on the right side, then make a hem large enough to allow the doweling to be slotted through. Slip stitch in place.

Decorate the hanging with ribbon, braid and tassels as preferred.

A Brooch and A Stationery Set

A pretty motif taken from the diaper design shown on the previous page and worked on a) very fine silk to make a brooch and b) on 14 count Aida and mounted in a stationery set. I have deliberately used two fabrics with very different counts to demonstrate how this can change the appearance of a design. If you are making the brooch, try to get silk which is pre-stretched onto a firm board, as it is impossible to work unless it is held taut. If the pre-stretched variety is unobtainable, use a small hoop frame.

METHOD

Fold the Aida in half lengthwise and crosswise to find the centre point; measure the silk. Crease or mark lightly. Start work at this point following the stitch marked on the chart on the right.

Work in cross stitch using one strand of cotton worked over one thread intersection for the silk and three strands over one intersection for the Aida.

When the stitching is completed, remove the mount from the silk and press the Aida gently from the wrong side. Trim and mount the pieces following the manufacturer's instructions.

MATERIALS

1 piece of white silk, 30 count, 4 x 4 in (10 x 10 cm), for the brooch (see page 93 for stockists)

1 piece of cream Aida, 14 count, 6 x 6 in (15 x 15 cm), for the stationery set

very fine tapestry needle, size 28 or higher, for the silk

tapestry needle, size 24, for the Aida

1 brooch mount (see page 93 for stockists)

1 stationery set (see page 93 for stockists)

1 skein each of stranded cotton in the following shades:

		DMC	Anchor
■	purple	550	101
▨	bronze	370	856

Finished size of design, silk: 1 1/4 x 1 3/4 in (3 x 4.5 cm)

Finished size of design, Aida: 3 x 3 5/8 in (7.5 x 9.2 cm)

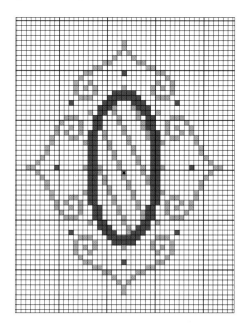

◆ **The same design used on different fabrics produces two quite different effects.**

MATERIALS

To make a set of four:

1 set of 4 white Sal-Em napkins, 26 count (see page 93 for stockists)

tapestry needle, size 24

2 skeins each of stranded cotton in the following shades:

		DMC	Anchor
	pink	605	50
	mauve	340	118
	green	563	208

4 skeins of stranded cotton in:

	yellow	445	288

Finished size of design (single unit):
⅞ x 2¼ in (2.2 x 7 cm)

Napkins

Border detail taken from the transfiguration and Last Supper illustration of the Florette Bible, dated c. 1156, and also used on the Band Sampler on page 41, provides the design for some table linen. The motifs can be worked as shown here, or just in the corners.

METHOD

Count eight threads up from the fray-stop line of stitching at the bottom of the napkin and eight threads in from the stitching line at the side. Begin work on the border design at this point following the starting stitch marked on the chart opposite.

Work in cross stitch using three strands of cotton over two threads of the fabric.

To work the centre motif, fold the napkin in half lengthwise and crosswise and crease lightly to find the centre point. Match this to the centre of the motif and start stitching at this point.

When the stitching is complete, press the fabric gently from the wrong side (see page 90).

◆ Far left: A border design for a napkin translated directly from a border in an illuminated Bible.

Left: A page from the Florette Bible dating from the mid 12th century, from which the border design was taken.

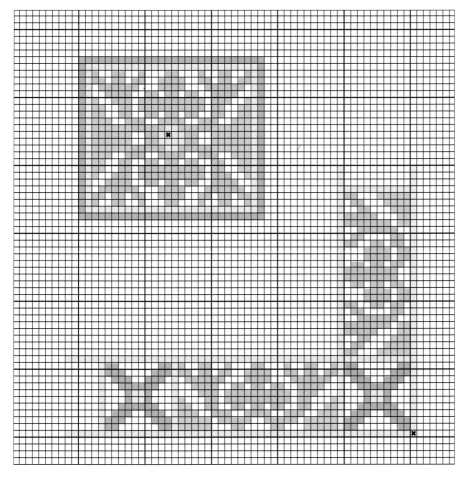

◆ Choose your own initial to make a charming, personalised picture.

Initial Letter

This project demonstrates the adaptability and interchangeability of the designs within this book. Here, one of the letters from the Alphabet Sampler on page 50 has been lifted out and surrounded by one of the borders from the Band Sampler on page 41. The frame below is shown as a square but can be extended in either direction if a larger central space is required.

METHOD

Measure 1 ½ in (4 cm) down from the top right corner of the fabric and 1 ½ in (4 cm) in from the righthand side. Begin work at this point following the starting stitch marked on the chart below.

Use two strands of cotton, working over one thread intersection. Work the border outline in backstitch, the rest in cross stitch. On completion of the border, work your chosen letter in the middle. Position the letter centrally by finding the centre of the fabric (fold into four and crease lightly) and counting to find the centre stitch of the initial. Begin in the middle of the fabric with this stitch.

When the stitching is completed, wash if necessary and press gently from the wrong side (see page 90).

For finishing and mounting as a little picture, see page 92.

MATERIALS

1 piece of white Aida, 18 count, 8 x 8 in (20 x 20 cm)

tapestry needle, size 24

1 skein each of stranded cotton in the following shades:

		DMC	Anchor
	purple	553	98
	red	349	13
	green	502	877
	mauve	554	97

plus the shades needed for the letter of your choice (see chart on pages 51-5)

Finished size of project: 4 ¼ x 4 ½ in (11 x 11.5 cm)

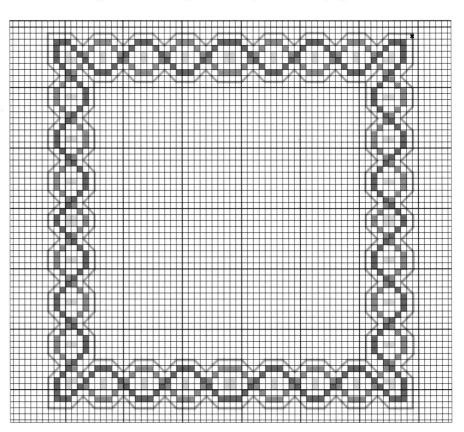

Alphabet Sampler

Inspired by the decorated initials of illuminated manuscripts from the medieval period, this is a large alphabet project. The motifs are derived from tapestry work, stained glass and the manuscripts themselves. The individual letters of the alphabet are a very useful design source for personalising other pieces of work, perhaps using the internal border as a framework. Alternatively, groups of initials could be worked together.

Most of the designs from manuscripts have been taken from various Books of Hours written in the later medieval period. These were small volumes of beautifully illustrated pages, commissioned either for personal use or as a gift and were usually used for private worship. They were treasured possessions and as a consequence many have survived.

The text featured popular religious and secular stories divided into episodes, each densely and finely illustrated often with a small inset picture in one corner. The figures in the pictures were often painted in contemporary fashion and thus give an excellent insight into the dress and activities of the time.

The French and Flemish painters of Books of Hours, in particular, were noted for their skill in illustrating realistic plants and flower heads. Lucky the lady who owned such a beautiful book!

◆ A page from a French Book of Hours showing an ornate letter D and various other plants which have inspired the designs for some of the letters in the highly decorative sampler shown on page 54.

51

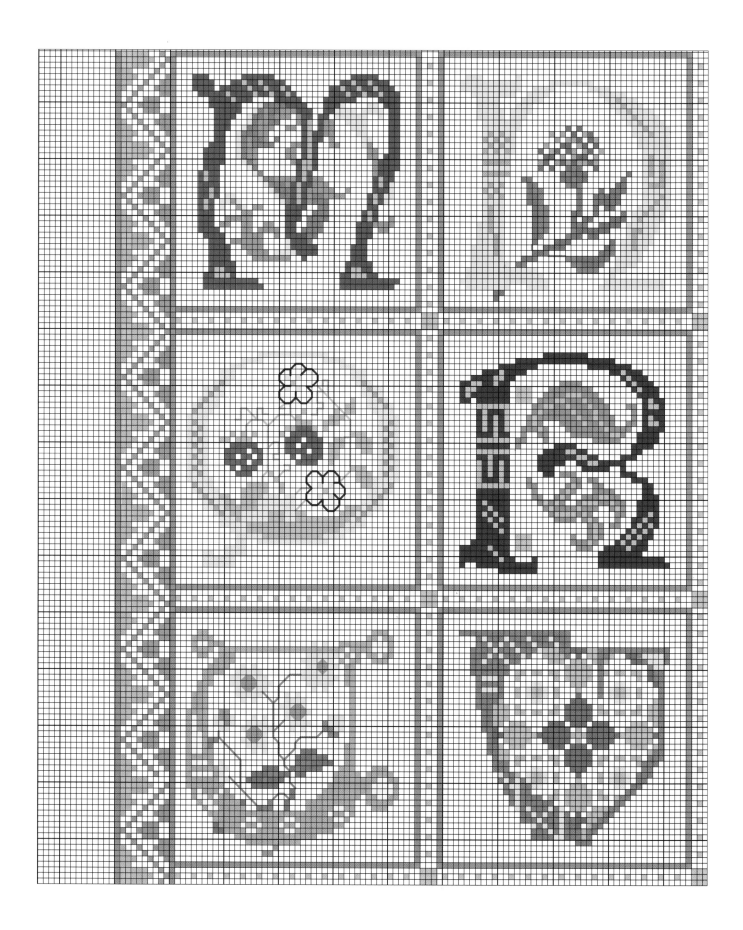

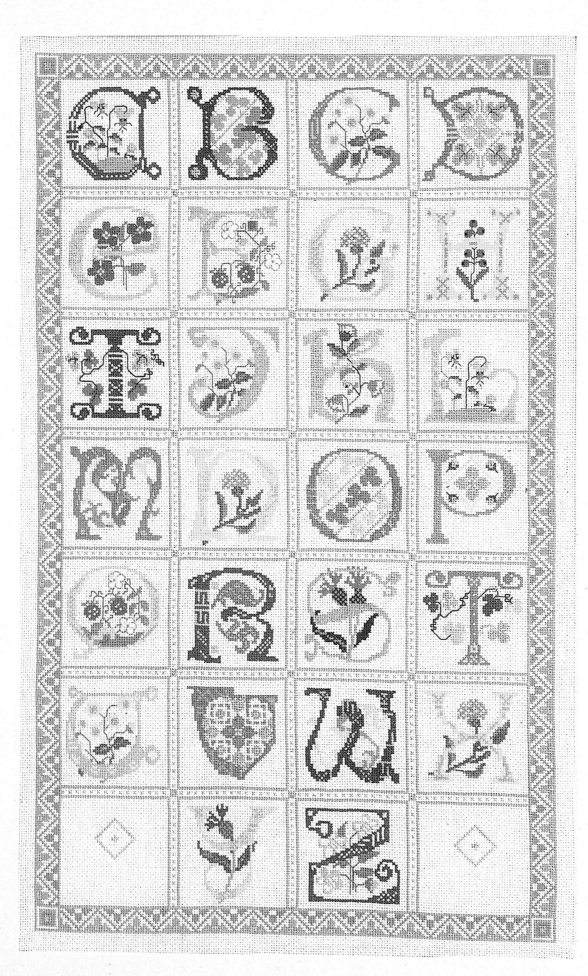

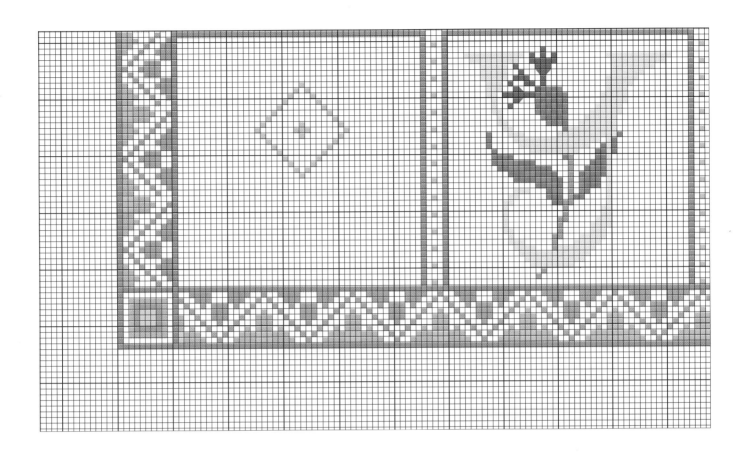

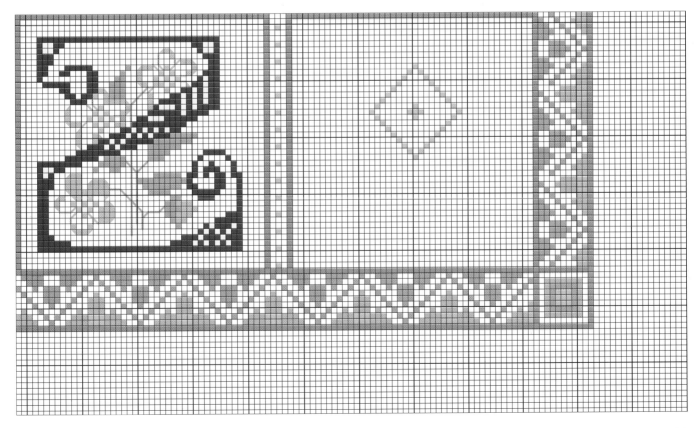

METHOD

As with the other detailed projects, I strongly recommend that you hem or tack the raw edges of the fabric before starting to cross stitch, in order to prevent fraying (see page 90).

Fold the fabric in half lengthwise to find the centre vertical line and crease lightly. Now measure down this fold for 3 in (7.5 cm) from the top of the fabric. This will give the point at which you start stitching on the fabric. Find the starting stitch marked on the chart on page 50 and begin work on the fabric with this stitch.

Use two strands of cotton, working over one thread intersection. Work all straight line detail in backstitch, the rest in cross stitch.

Work either from left to right or vice versa. Stitch the horizontal border line almost to the end - it is easier to add a few stitches than to unpick excess ones. Next work the central vertical border using the same 'fall short' principle. Work the letters 'B' and 'C' on either side of this vertical, then the horizontal line under these letters. Continue to build up the design in this way.

The two blank squares at the base are for you to personalise with your name or initials and date of working. Refer to the Heraldic Shield Sampler on pages 36-7 for the letter shapes and to page 92 for information on how to position them.

For finishing and mounting instructions, see page 92.

◆ Designs for the alphabet sampler were inspired by the strawberries, curly leaves, violas and other flowers from this lovely Book of Hours (left), while the lattice border comes from another page from the same book (above).

MATERIALS

1 piece of white Aida, 16 count, 20 x 28 in (51 x 71 cm)

tapestry needle, size 26

lightweight wadding for mounting (optional)

1 skein each of stranded cotton in the following shades, unless otherwise stated:

	DMC	Anchor
greens		
	367	216
	470	266
	471	265
	472	278
	500	879
	501	878
	502	877
	563	208
	564	206
	580	924
	597	168
	988	243

	991	189
	3347	266
pinks and purples		
	211	342
	327	100
	554	97
	604	55
	605	50
(2 skeins)	962	75
	3687	68
(3 skeins)	899	40
yellows		
	726	295
	727	293
	3078	292
browns and greys		
	318	399
(5 skeins)	833	907
	3064	883
	3772	914

blues		
	792	177
	793	176
	799	145
	800	144
	809	130
reds and peaches		
	347	13
	349	19
	353	6
white		
border shades		
light brown	833	907
dark pink	962	75
blue	799	145
gold metallic (2 skeins)		

Finished size of design: 13 x 21½ in (33 x 54.5 cm)

◆ A little pincushion using one of the motifs from the Alphabet Sampler.

Pincushion

A small project and a good way of using up leftover pieces of fabric. The design source is from the illuminated manuscripts which make great use of this ivy-leaf motif and tendrils. The same design is used to decorate two of the letters in the Alphabet Sampler on page 54. Use this little cushion for your tapestry needles (see page 91): how much simpler it is to stitch a large design when we have a needle for every shade!

METHOD

Fold one of the pieces of Aida in half lengthwise and crosswise to find the centre point. Crease lightly. Start work at this point following the stitch marked on the chart below.

Use three strands of cotton worked over one thread intersection. Work the leaf stems in backstitch, the rest in cross stitch.

When the stitching is complete, press the fabric gently from the wrong side. Place the two pieces of Aida right sides together and machine stitch or back stitch by hand around three sides of the square, leaving a ¼ in (6 mm) hem. Trim the corners, then turn right side out. Fill the cushion with the stuffing to the desired density, then turn under the seam allowance on the open side and slip stitch to close.

Stitch the braid around all four edges of the cushion, tucking the ends into the seam allowance and attach tassels if using.

MATERIALS

2 pieces of cream Aida, 14 count, each 4 x 4 in (10 x 10 cm)

tapestry needle, size 24

polyester stuffing

4 tassels (optional)

braid 18 in (45 cm) in length

1 skein each of stranded cotton in the following shades:

		DMC	Anchor
	blue	809	130
	dark peach	352	9
	light peach	353	6
	green	563	208

Finished size of design: 2¼ x 2¼ in (5.5 x 5.5 cm)

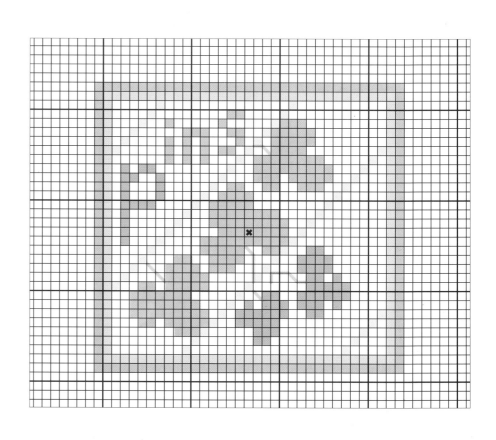

A Money Box and A Wooden Pot

A very small design taken from the border surrounding a painting of Ernest of Pardubice (the first Archbishop of Prague) adoring God the Father in an illuminated manuscript of the 14th century. Illuminated manuscripts are a rich source for motifs of all sizes. Small studies like this are extremely versatile: they can either be used singly, as in this design, or they can be used severally as corner motifs in a rectangular border; or repeated in a strip to form a bookmark design.

MATERIALS

2 pieces of white Aida, 14 count, each 4 x 4 in (10 x 10 cm)

tapestry needle, size 24

1 card money box (see page 93 for stockists)

1 wooden pot, 3 in (7.5 cm) diameter lid (see page 93 for stockists)

fabric adhesive

1 skein each of stranded cotton in the following shades:

		DMC	Anchor
	pink	605	50
	yellow	726	295
	blue	340	118

Finished size of design: 1¼ x 1¼ in (3 x 3 cm)

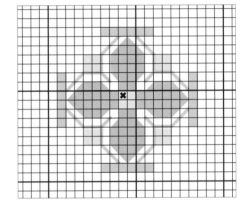

◆ Above: A small, stylised flower motif forming the corner of a border in a Czech prayer book from the 14th century.
Above left: Two alternative uses of this decorative device.

METHOD

Work as follows for both pieces.
Fold the Aida in half lengthwise and crosswise to find the centre point. Crease lightly. Start work at this point following the stitch marked on the chart on the right.

Use three strands of cotton over one thread intersection, either repeating the motif exactly on each piece or changing the base shade. Work the outline detail in backstitch, the rest in cross stitch.

When the stitching is completed, press gently from the wrong side, then mount according to the manufacturer's instructions.

Strawberry Bookmark

MATERIALS

1 lacy bookmark (see page 93 for stockists)

tapestry needle, size 26

1 skein each of stranded cotton in the following shades:

		DMC	Anchor
	yellow	743	305
	green	988	243
	brown	436	363
	red	347	13
	grey	413	401

Finished size of design: 1¼ x 5½ in (3 x 14 cm)

Strawberry plants seem to have had a very special place in the hearts and minds of the medieval illuminators as examples are to be found spinning their fruits and flowers through many a page! This design is an adaptation of one such illumination, from a French Book of Hours. The design has been elongated so that it will fit onto the bookmark but could easily be broken into sections to be used on cards, gift tags, etc.

METHOD

Fold the bookmark in half lengthwise to find the centre vertical line and mark this at the top with a pin. Check the number of threads per inch on the bookmark against the chart on page 61. The bookmark counts can vary by one or two squares; if there is a discrepancy, adjust the design accordingly, so that it is centred on the bookmark. Count down the same number of threads on the fabric as there are squares on the design chart (allowing for any discrepancy) and begin work with the starting stitch given on the chart.

The back stitch round the strawberry flowers is worked using one strand of grey over one thread intersection, two strands are used everywhere else.

When the stitching is completed, wash if necessary and press gently from the wrong side (see page 90).

◆ A French Book of Hours painted c.1470 provides one of the many examples of strawberries among an abundance of other flowers.

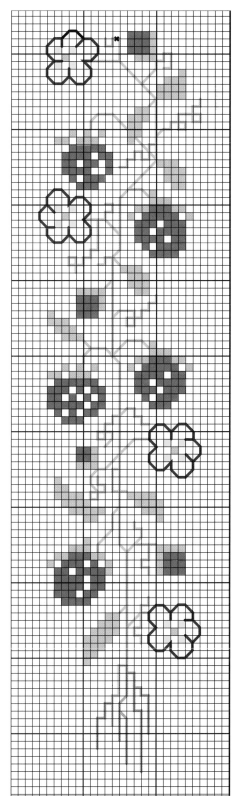

◆ An embroidered book cover and a floral bookmark make two very attractive gifts for book lovers.

MATERIALS

*1 piece of cream Aida, 16 count, 8 x 8 in
(20 x 20 cm)*

tapestry needle, size 26

*1 piece of iron-on interfacing, same
size as Aida*

*fabric for book cover, e.g. heavy cotton, velvet
(see method)*

large piece of scrap paper

1 yard (1 metre) braid (optional)

*1 skein each of stranded cotton in the
following shades:*

		DMC	Anchor
	green	988	243
	bronze	834	874
	beige	677	300
	gold metallic		

2 skeins of stranded cotton in:

	pale green	369	213

*Finished size of design: 4¾ x 5 in
(12 x 12.5 cm)*

Book Cover

A panel of 14th century woven silk and gilt from Sicily or Northern Italy forms the basis for this square design which can be used complete, as here, for a book cover or on place mats. The two parts of the design, i.e. the central motif and the border, could also be used independently of each other.

METHOD

Fold the Aida in half lengthwise and crosswise to find the centre point. Crease lightly. Start work at this point following the stitch marked on the chart on page 63.

Work in cross stitch using three strands of cotton over one thread intersection.

When the stitching is completed, press lightly from the wrong side, then turn under the unworked fabric all round, trim and stitch down. Place the interfacing centrally on the reverse of the work, trim it so that it is just a little shorter all round, then iron in place.

This panel can now be attached to a book cover you can make from contrasting fabric. Wrap the paper around the book you wish to cover and make a pattern, including book flaps. Add ½ in (12 mm) hem allowance to all edges. Cut out the fabric to this pattern. Turn under the ½ in (12 mm) hem and stitch down. Place in position round the book and pin the cross-stitched panel to the front of the cover in the desired position. Slip stitch neatly in place and, if you so wish, add braid round the edges. Finally slip stitch the book flaps to form pockets for the book covers.

◆ A detail from the finely-woven Italian
cloth which served as the inspiration
for the book cover design.

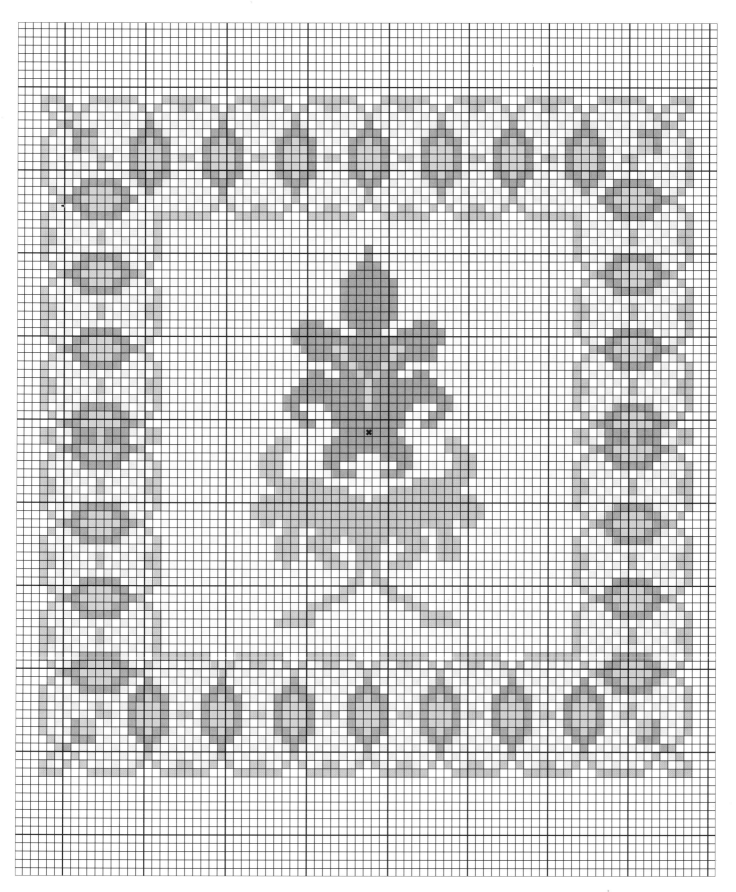

MATERIALS

To make a 16 in (40 cm) square cushion cover:

1 piece of white Aida, 11 count, 18 x 18 in (45 x 45 cm)

1 piece of iron-on interfacing, same size as Aida

1 piece of cotton fabric for the back of the cover, 18 x 18 in (45 x 45 cm)

tapestry needle, size 22 or 24

1 cushion pad, 16 x 16 in (40 x 40 cm)

2 yards (2 metres) braid (optional)

2 skeins each of stranded cotton in the following shades:

		DMC	Anchor
yellows			
	inner	783	307
	middle	725	306
	outer	727	29
pinks			
	inner	3687	68
	middle	3688	66
	outer	3689	49
greens			
	inner	911	230
	middle	913	204
	outer	955	206
purples			
	inner	208	111
	middle	209	109
	outer	211	342
flower centres			
	brown	3064	883

Finished size of design: 8 ³/₄ x 6 ¹/₂ in (22 x 16.5 cm)

◆ **A highly adaptable repeat design has here been made into a colourful cushion.**

Cushion

A detail from the Psalter of Henry of Blois gives the basis for a repeat design that can be reproduced in almost every size imaginable. The psalter (a personal prayer book) was made in the middle of 12th century at Winchester for the bishop, Henry of Blois, who was a committed patron of the arts. The psalter depicts scenes from both the Old and New Testaments.

This design can be used wherever a solidly stitched panel is required. Using different shades will also completely change the design's effect, as demonstrated on this cushion cover.

METHOD

Fold the Aida in half lengthwise and crosswise to find the centre point. Crease lightly. Start work at this point following the stitch marked on the chart on page 65.

Work in cross stitch using four strands of cotton over one thread intersection.

When the stitching is completed, press gently from the wrong side. Place the embroidery and the cotton fabric for the back with right sides together. Pin and machine stitch or back stitch by hand along the border of the stitching, making a 2 in (5 cm) seam and leaving part of one side open. Trim the seam to ¹/₂ in (12 mm) and across the corners. Turn right side out. Insert the cushion pad into the cover, then turn under the remaining raw edges and slip stitch the opening together. Decorate the edges as you wish.

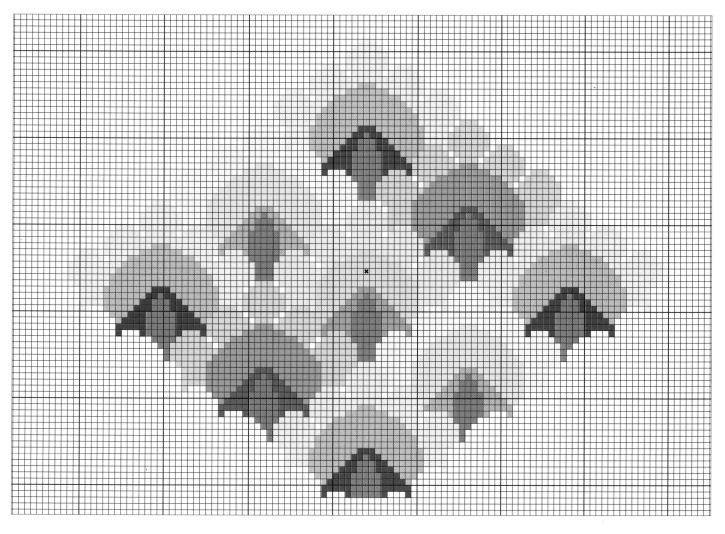

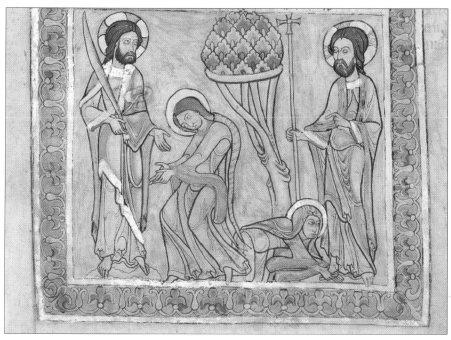

◆ The stylised tree provides a ready
motif for stitching.

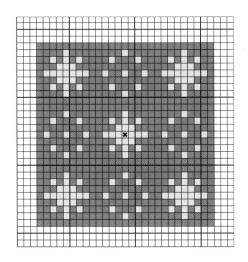

Greetings Card and A Notepaper Block

Two diaper designs from 14th century illuminated manuscripts form the basis for these pretty projects. Diaper is the name given in this context to the ornamentation of background or walls. Many of the manuscripts contain pictures within the main picture and these pictures-within-pictures often had very ornate, delicate background decoration.

These motifs could be used just as effectively as pincushion patterns or made into a larger design by repeating the blocks butting one to the next or by using another single line of stitches in a contrasting colour to separate and link each block.

METHOD

Work as follows for both designs. Fold the Aida in half lengthwise and crosswise to find the centre point. Crease lightly. Start work at this point following the stitch marked on the relevant chart on the left or below.

Use three strands of cotton over one thread intersection. Work the outline detail in backstitch, the rest in cross stitch.

When the stitching is completed, mount the card and the notepaper block following the instructions on page 92.

MATERIALS

4 pieces of white Aida, 14 count, 5 x 5 in (12.5 x 12.5 cm)

tapestry needle, size 24

1 card blank (see page 93 for stockists)

1 noteblock (see page 93 for stockists)

fabric adhesive

lightweight wadding for mounting (optional)

1 skein each of stranded cotton in the following shades:

		DMC	Anchor
	green	911	230
	blue	798	131
	red	666	46
	yellow	444	291
	gold metallic		

Finished size (both designs): 2 x 2 in (5 x 5 cm)

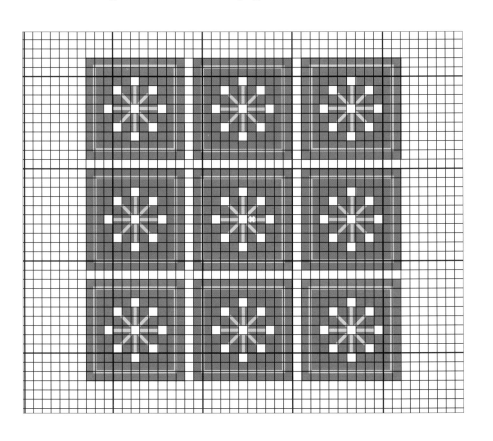

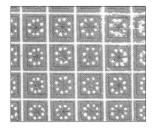

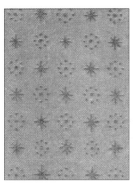

◆ Above: Two small designs make stationery special.

Left: A close-up of the two diaper patterns from medieval manuscripts which inspired the stationery designs.

◆ Right: Two-colour floor tiles were the most typical product of the medieval tiler.

Below: Two treatments of the fleur-de-lys motif: to fit a long, thin design and a circular area.

A Desk Pen Set and A Band Design

Two designs using encaustic tiles of the 14th century as source material. Encaustic is the name given to the art of inlaying by burning-in different coloured clays into the base.

METHOD

For the pen set design, fold the Aida in half lengthwise and crosswise to find the centre point. Crease lightly. Start work at this point following the stitch marked on the chart below. For the band design, first decide on the length of band required, then fold lengthwise and crosswise to find the centre point. Work one of the motifs at this point following the start stitch on the chart below right. Work the next motifs on either side as mirror images of the first, leaving one stitch unworked in between.

MATERIALS

1 piece of white Aida, 18 count, 6 x 6 in (15 x 15 cm), for the desk pen set

1 piece of white Aida band, 4 in (10 cm) wide, to your required length

tapestry needle, size 24 or 26

1 desk pen set (see page 93 for stockists)

1 skein each of stranded cotton in the following shades:

		DMC	Anchor
desk pen set			
▢ yellow		972	298
▨ dark red		498	43
▧ blue		311	148
band design			
▨ blue		798	131
▢ yellow		444	291

Finished size of design (pen set): 2 ¼ x 2 ¼ in (5.5 x 5.5 cm)

Finished size of single design (band): 2 x 1 ⅞ in (5 x 4.8 cm)

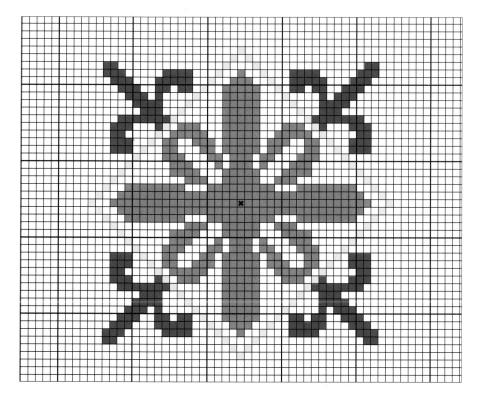

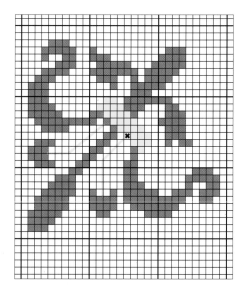

Continue in this way, alternately reversing the motifs.

Use three strands of cotton over one thread intersection. Work the outline detail in backstitch, the rest in cross stitch.

When the stitching is complete, press the fabric gently from the wrong side and mount the design for the desk pen set following the manufacturer's instructions.

A Door Finger Panel and a Tablecloth

This rose is adapted from one which appears on the border of a 1458 tapestry, entitled, 'Auguste et la Sibylle'. It can be worked singly for pot lids or greetings cards, in rows for table linen, or as a sampler border. Try experimenting with other shades, using the depth tones of its pink rose as your guide.

The design is shown here in two versions. Firstly, on a door finger panel, in a repeat pattern where every alternate rose is reversed; secondly, on a circular tablecloth for an occasional table. If you wish to undertake this second project, the rose needs to be modified to fit the evenweave circles on the fabric. To do this, omit the main rose and stem and stitch only the buds and leaves.

◆ Right: 'Auguste et la Sibylle': a mid 15th century tapestry woven in Brussels.
Far right: Two alternative treatments of the same rose motif.

Materials

1 piece of white Aida, 18 count, 12 x 4 ½ in (30 x 11.5 cm), for the door panel

1 piece of iron-on interfacing, same size as Aida, for the door panel

'Schonfells' damask fabric, 55 in (140 cm) wide (see method), for the tablecloth (see page 93 for stockists)

tapestry needle, size 26

door protector blank (see page 93 for stockists)

1 skein each of stranded cotton in the following shades:

		DMC	Anchor
	pink	3716	25
	medium pink	961	76
	dark pink	962	75
	green	368	214
	medium green	987	244
	dark green	895	269

Finished size of design, door finger panel: 1 ¾ x 6 in (4.5 x 15 cm)

Finished size of single design, tablecloth: 2 ¼ x 3 in (5.5 x 7.5 cm)

Method

To make the door finger panel, fold the Aida in half lengthwise and crosswise to find the centre point. Crease lightly. Start work at this point following the stitch marked on the chart below. Stitch the motifs on either side, reversing the image and starting on the same line as the last stitch of the first motif.

Work in cross stitch using two strands of cotton over one thread intersection.

When the stitching is completed, wash if necessary and press gently from the wrong side (see page 90). Place the interfacing centrally on the reverse of the work and iron in position. Trim the fabric to fit the door protector blank, using the front as a template. Complete according to manufacturer's instructions.

To make the round tablecloth, you will first need to measure the table it is to cover and, unless you do not mind a join, 55 in (140 cm) is the maximum width possible. First measure the distance from the edge of the table to the floor, or to wherever you wish the overhang to finish. Double this measurement and add it to the diameter of the table top. Add a further 1 in (2.5 cm) for the hem allowance. This measurement gives you the length of fabric required and as it is for a circular cloth, it is also the measurement for the width. Cut a square of fabric to these measurements, then fold the fabric into four, wrong side out.

Now halve the measurement and cut a square of scrap paper with sides to this size. Lay the paper flat on a surface you do not mind a drawing pin being stuck into. Tie a length of string or thread to a pencil and push a drawing pin through it at the same distance from the pencil as the radius of the tablecloth plus the seam allowance (i.e. half the original measurement). Stick the drawing pin into one corner of the paper and, with the string pulled taut, draw an arc or quarter circle from one edge of the paper to the other. Cut this out and use as a paper pattern on your fabric, placing the curved side of the pattern towards the edges of the fabric and the corner where the drawing pin was into the folded corner of the fabric. Cut along the curve.

Preparation complete, you can now start to stitch the rose buds, one in each of the circular evenweave insets, deciding beforehand whether you wish them to all face the same way, be upright, rotate or alternatively reverse. Use three strands of cotton over one thread intersection.

On completion, rinse if necessary, hem the edge of the cloth and gently press.

Small Picture

The lily motif is taken from a detail on a stained glass window entitled, 'The Virgin and the Child'. Made in c. 1480 in the workshop of Peter Hemmel for Kloster Nonnburg in Salzburg, Austria, it is a lovely example of the development in design towards more natural images which was taking place at this time.

The lily, like the rose of the previous project, is a useful motif to have in one's pattern book, as it is highly adaptable.

MATERIALS

1 piece of cream Aida, 16 count, 8 x 11 in (20 x 28 cm)

tapestry needle, size 26

lightweight wadding for mounting (optional)

picture frame, 8 x 6 in (20 x 15 cm)

1 skein each of stranded cotton in the following shades:

		DMC	Anchor
	green	3348	264
	pale pink	3689	49
	pink	3688	66
	dark green	3347	266
	yellow	726	295
	brown	738	361

Finished size: 3 x 4⅞ in (7.5 x 12.4 cm)

METHOD

Fold the fabric in half lengthwise to find the centre vertical line and crease lightly. Now measure down this fold for 2 in (5 cm) from the top of the fabric. This will give the point at which you start stitching on the fabric. Find the starting stitch marked on the chart on page 75 and begin work on the fabric with this stitch.

Work in cross stitch using two strands of cotton over one thread intersection. Outline the flowers in back stitch.

When the stitching is completed, wash if necessary and press gently from the wrong side (see page 90). Trim and mount in the picture frame, using wadding in between the embroidery and the backing board if liked (see page 92).

◆ **A pretty botanical illustration to hang on your wall.**

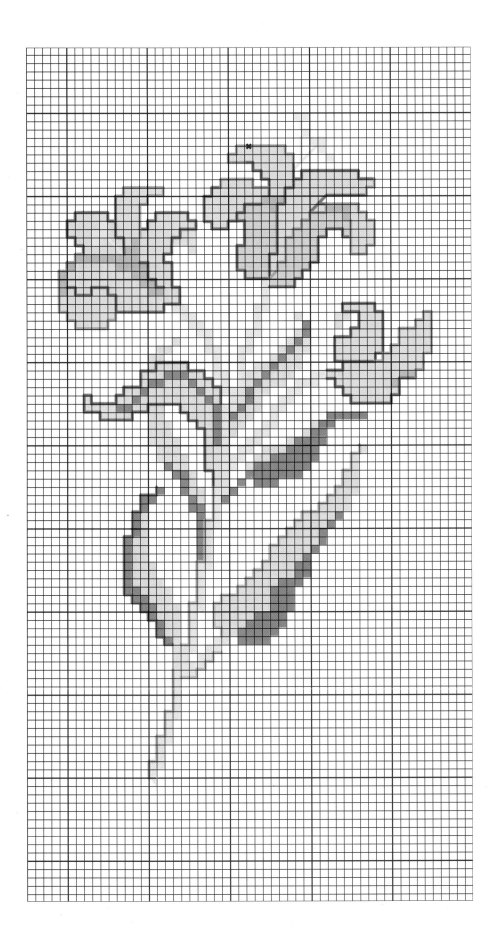

◆ Left: The picture lily was inspired by this wonderfully vibrant stained glass panel in an Austrian church.

MATERIALS

2 pieces of cream Aida, 18 count,
6 ½ x 4 ½ in (16 x 11.5 cm), for design A

2 piece of white Aida, 22 count, 6 ½ x 4 ½ in
(16 x 11.5 cm), for design B

tapestry needle, size 26

2 lengths of narrow ribbon or braid,
12 in (30 cm) long

pot pourri mixture or dried lavender

1 skein each of stranded cotton in the
following shades:

		DMC	Anchor
design A			
	yellow	727	293
	dark yellow	676	891
	pink	605	50
	bright pink	603	62
	blue	809	130
	green	564	206
design B			
	gold metallic		
	green	368	214

Finished size, design A: 2 ½ x 2 ½ in
(6 x 6 cm)

Finished size, design B: 1 ½ x 1 ⅞ in
(4 x 4.5 cm)

Two Pot Pourri Bags

Two motifs inspired by a 14th century Swiss linen tablecloth, the original worked in blocked satin, brick and interlacing whitework, and adapted here for simple cross-stitch projects, when a small, cross-shaped motif might be required. The Swiss tablecloth was intended for secular use but whitework was also used in the church on the large Lenten veils that would conceal the high altar during Lent.

Although they have been used singly here, both designs would adapt well to a border design for a sampler or to a strip pattern for a cake band.

METHOD

Work as follows for both designs.

With the short sides at top and bottom, fold the Aida in half lengthwise to find the centre vertical line and crease lightly. Measure 1 in (2.5 cm) up this line from the bottom for design A and 1 ¼ in (3 cm) up this line for design B. Start work at this point following the stitch marked on the relevant chart below or on the right.

Work in cross stitch using two strands of cotton over one thread intersection when stitching design A and one strand of cotton over one thread intersection for design B.

Two make up the pot pourri bag, place an embroidered piece of fabric on top of an unworked piece with right sides together. Machine stitch or back stitch by hand round two long sides and the short side nearest to the motif, leaving a ¼ in (6 mm) seam allowance. Trim the corners, then turn through to the right side. Turn under a hem on the remaining raw edges and stitch down. Fill three-quarters full with a pot pourri mixture or dried lavender, then tie with the ribbon at the top to enclose the pot pourri.

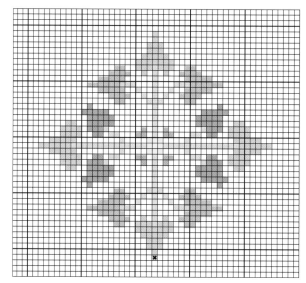

design A

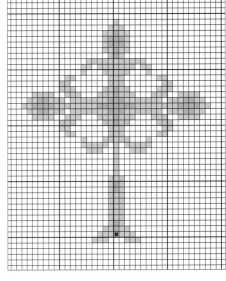

design B

◆ Above: This intricately embroidered
Swiss cloth provides a variety
of motifs which can be adapted to
cross stitch.
Left: Pot pourri bags make
useful little gifts.

◆ The geometric design of this 15th century Spanish silk translates well into cross stitch.

Clock

Woven silk with laceria design work from the 15th century, Spanish in origin, is the source for this project. Laceria is a geometric pattern which resembles interwoven canework. Luxurious woven silks were produced in Spain from the 10th century onwards. Centres were to be found throughout the country, including at Seville, Granada and Almeria.

This geometric motif could be used wherever a squarer, more angular shape is required: on its own, repeated horizontally or vertically, or worked in blocks with a 'fill-in' colour between.

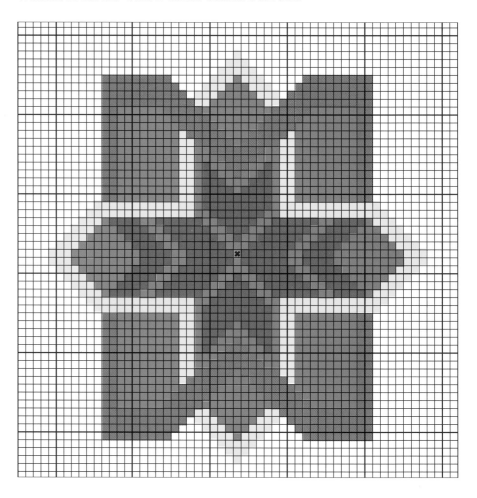

MATERIALS

1 piece of white Aida, 14 count, 5 x 6 in (12.5 x 15 cm)

tapestry needle, size 24

1 clock set (see page 93 for stockists)

1 skein each of stranded cotton in the following shades:

		DMC	Anchor
	blue	792	177
	yellow	444	291
	green	700	228
	red	666	46

Finished size: 3 x 3¼ in (7.5 x 8 cm)

METHOD

Fold the Aida in half lengthwise and crosswise to find the centre point. Crease lightly. Start work at this point following the stitch marked on the chart above.

Work in cross stitch using two strands of cotton over one thread intersection.

When the stitching is complete, press gently from the wrong side, then mount according to the manufacturer's instructions.

Wooden-based Pincushion

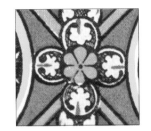

A detail taken from a stained glass window in Soissons Cathedral gives this quatrefoil shaped design. It is only a little portion of a much larger window design and I have used it to demonstrate that even a tiny section of a full design is capable of standing alone as a complete motif. Next time you visit a building with stained glass, take time to look not only at the overall effect, but also at each part of the design, isolating it from the rest. I am sure you will be inspired to rush out and get a sketchbook to note some ideas to try out at home!

METHOD

Fold the Aida into four to find the centre point. Crease lightly. Start work at this point following the stitch marked on the chart on the right.

Work in cross stitch using two strands of cotton over one thread intersection.

When the stitching is completed, wash if necessary and press gently from the wrong side (see page 90). Thread the sharp needle with sewing thread and run a gathering stitch round the Aida, 1/4 (6 mm) in from the edge. Pull up loosely into a bag. Fill three-quarters full with the stuffing, slip in the card circle, then pull up the gathers tightly, tucking the raw edges inside the bag as you do so. Knot the thread, then oversew to secure. Touch the base with adhesive or use a small piece of double-sided Sellotape and sit the pincushion in its base.

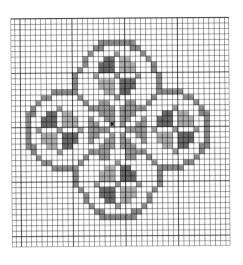

MATERIALS

1 piece of cream Aida, 18 count, 8 in (20 cm) in diameter

1 piece of iron-on interfacing, same size as Aida

tapestry needle, size 26

polyester stuffing

fabric adhesive or double-sided Sellotape

sharp needle and cream sewing thread

1 pincushion base, 3 1/4 in (8 cm) in diameter (see page 93 for stockists)

circle of lightweight card, 3 1/4 in (8 cm) in diameter

1 skein each of stranded cotton in the following shades:

		DMC	Anchor
	green	471	265
	dark green	469	267
	purple	327	100
	bronze or gold metallic		

Finished size of design: 2 x 2 in (5 x 5 cm)

◆ Two geometric designs from quite different sources.

Chart-only samplers

This last section features original source material linked to fully charted adaptations for you to stitch into complete samplers. The photographs represent three important aspects of medieval art: a beautifully painted Book of Hours; the famous Bayeux Tapestry and a vividly coloured stained glass window.

These pieces can be stitched by following the charts exactly and will make stunning samplers in their own right. Alternatively, they can be adapted to your own requirements or split up and used as a motif library. Details on how to estimate the size of fabric required are given on page 92.

PAGES 81 TO 82

BAYEUX TAPESTRY SAMPLER

This photograph shows a small section of the famous Bayeux Tapestry, a mammoth piece of embroidery which is 193 feet (over 70 metres) long and tells the story of the conquest of England by William the Conqueror. It was worked in France in the eleventh century. This section shows the ships carrying William's army complete with horses to Pevensey. The chart could be extended by adding more border detail at the top and sides. I suggest you work on a buff or ecru coloured fabric, so that the white stitching shows up. The back stitch detail for the faces is left for you to add if desired.

PAGES 83 TO 85

BOOK OF HOURS SAMPLER

This exquisite page is taken from a Book of Hours illuminated in the Netherlands in the late fifteenth century. The artist is 'The Master of Mary of Burgundy' known after the owner of the book. This page is part of the illustration surrounding a prayer to St Anthony Abbot who lived as a hermit. The chart leaves the central area blank for you to personalise to make a striking commemorative sampler. Details on letter spacing are given on page 92. The cornflowers and butterflies also provide very pretty designs to add to your motif library.

PAGES 86 TO 88

STAINED GLASS PANEL SAMPLER

The medieval cathedral of Chartres in France has many fine stained glass panels and no fewer than three rose windows. This photograph shows a section from a window dedicated to the parable of the Good Samaritan. The central quatrefoil shape in the chart has been used as a frame for some of the flower motifs given elsewhere in the book. You could try working the design on blue fabric but if you prefer to work on white, fill in the background grid with blue stitches and leave the white stitches blank. Any other motifs could be stitched within the quatrefoil.

ET VENIT AD PEVE

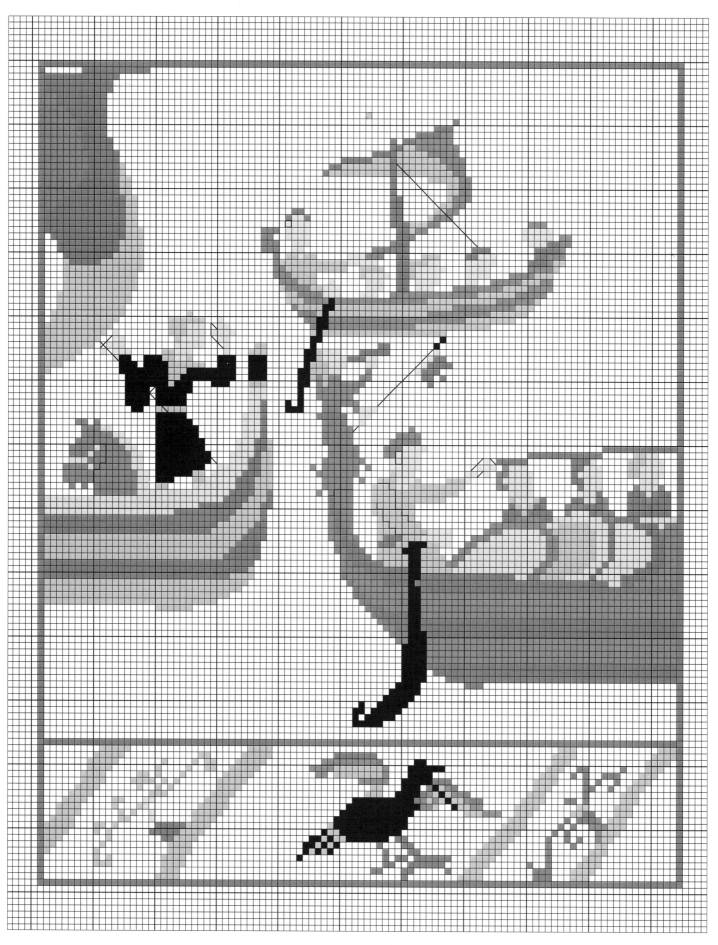

xi. versus. Ora pro
nobis beate pater
anthoni. ineternite
pestem epidimie il
lesi transire et pro
missiones xpristi
obtinere. oratio.
Deus qui con
cedis obtentu
beati anthonii con
fessoris tui morbi
dium ignent extin
gui et membris e
cris restituera psta

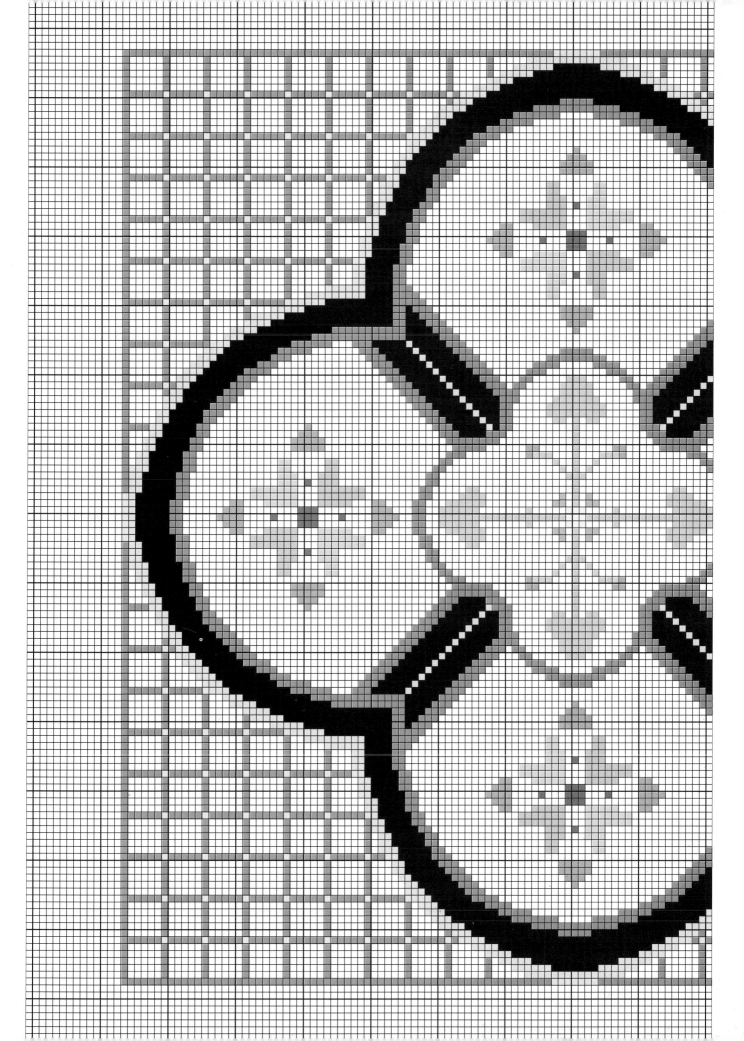

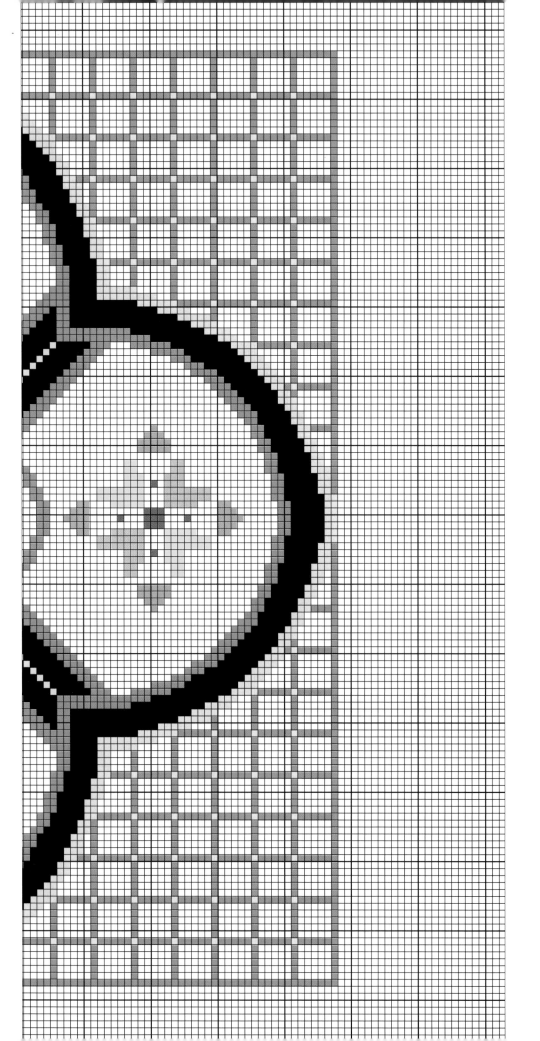

Practical Details

FABRICS

Cross stitch is mostly worked on evenweave fabrics - those which have a well-defined, equal warp (vertical) and weft (horizontal) thread, woven in such a way that there are the same number of warp as of weft threads in any square of fabric. Evenweave fabric comes in a variety of types and sizes, which are graded according to the number of threads or holes per inch with the highest number denoting the finest weave and consequently producing the finest stitch. This grading of fabric is referred to as the 'count' of the fabric, so that 18 count fabric will have 18 holes and threads to the inch (2.5 centimetres). Grades range from 10 count through to 26. If a novice, I suggest you start with projects on a lower count (14, for example) and when you are conversant with the basic skill move to the finer or higher counts.

Aida is a widely available type of evenweave fabric and many of the projects in this book are worked on it in various counts. It is woven with groups of warp and weft threads bulked together and woven as one unit, which leaves clearly defined holes between and makes it easy to see where to place the stitches.

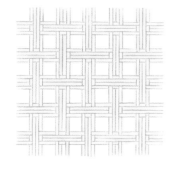

Hardanger, a type of evenweave in which pairs of threads are woven together, is also available and the same principles apply.

Lugana is another type of evenweave. A 25 count is available in a variety of shades and is a lovely fabric for bellpulls and wall hangings, as it is softer than Aida but weightier, so that it hangs well. It also has the advantage that, like linens, it can be worked over one or two threads.

Also featured in this book are products made from 'Sal-Em' fabric, an American-produced fabric, cut to the shape of napkins or traycloths with frayed edges and a pre-stitched line around the edges to prevent further fraying. It can be used either for fine stitches worked over one thread to form 26 count or over two threads to form 13 count. If unavailable, a 26 count linen could be used. You could, then, either hem or fray the edges yourself.

Linen is also suitable. This is a plain-weave, i.e. a fabric in which a single weft is woven alternately over and under a single warp, but is still suitable for cross-stitch work as the weaving of the warp and weft threads is equally spaced throughout the fabric.

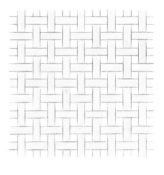

Special silk fabric is also used, this has a very high count and needs to be stretched into a frame, to make it manageable for stitching. It is available in pre-stretched form (see page 93) and is supplied with a fine needle. Make sure you are working in a good, bright light when stitching silk, as it is very fine work.

All the fabrics come in a variety of shades and colours. I have used mostly cream and white in this series, but do try experimenting with other shades. Maybe your specialist needlecraft store has a few remnant pieces you could try at not too high a cost for experimentation.

Waste canvas

Other fabrics can be used if your eye and patience are good, but do not attempt to use these until you have mastered the craft.

Waste canvas, available from specialist stores can help with the stitching of non-defined fabric, that is fabric which does not have an obvious grid of threads to work over, such as towelling or velvet. Waste canvas provides a temporary grid, which can be removed after it has been stitched over.

Pin or tack a piece of waste canvas 1 in (2.5 cm) larger all round than the design to be stitched onto the fabric you wish to embroider. Work your stitches over it but be careful not to pull up the stitches too tightly. Once the stitching is

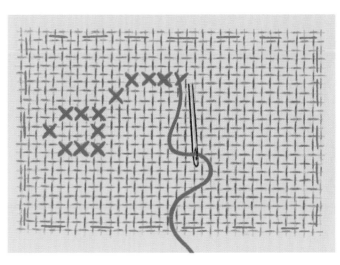

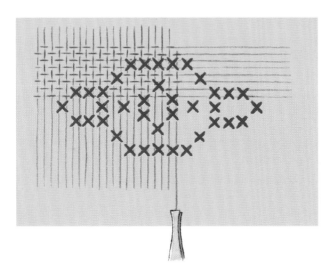

completed, draw out the threads of the waste canvas one by one with tweezers. They should release quite easily as long as your tension has not been too severe!

Care of fabric

All the evenweaves and linen launder beautifully and the stranded cottons used throughout the books are colourfast. If you are in any doubt about whether your threads are colourfast, do a test wash using a little of all the colours on a small piece first. When you have completed your project, if you feel it has become slightly grubby from handling, just wash gently in warm, soapy water, then rinse, to revitalise it. You will also be able to re-stiffen the evenweave Aida by doing this, which will make it easier to mount, as it does tend to soften while being worked. Roll up the embroidery in a dry towel to take out excess moisture, then leave the work on a flat surface to dry naturally. When dry, gently press the embroidery from the wrong side on a dry towel base with a medium-hot steam iron. The fabric can also be given a gentle press in this way during the stitching of a large project, if you feel it has become too limp.

THREADS

Every shade imaginable can be purchased! Half the fun is deciding which to use. Metallic threads are also popular and can add quite a sparkle to your work but the mainstay thread for cross stitch is stranded cotton. It is so-called because each thread is made up of six strands, which are separated to work with, the number of strands altering dependent on the count of the fabric.

As a rough guide on 10 to 14 count use three strands (unless the design is so dense you prefer to use two strands on 14); on 16 to 22 use two strands and on higher counts, one strand.

Other threads, such as crochet cotton, Danish flower threads, coton à broder and stranded silk are also suitable for cross stitch, though the thicker single strand threads should only be used on low counts of fabric.

Use of threads

As suggested, use different numbers of strands for different counts of fabric but universally do not thread your needle with more than a 14 in (35 cm) length at any time. A longer thread will eventually fray in the needle as it is drawn repeatedly through the fabric and leave a feathery thread on the stitching; it may, indeed, even fray out and break.

NEEDLES

Always use blunt-ended tapestry needles. The general rule regarding size is that the eye of the needle should be able to pass through the fabric without distorting the weave and leaving a larger hole. Size 24 is perfect for counts up to 14 and size 26 is fine for other higher counts; on silk use an even finer needle - size 28 or higher - as these are often up to 48 count!

FRAMES

Hoop frames are often used to prevent distortion of the fabric caused by an over-tight tension. Try a small one if you wish, your needlecraft shop will advise you and let you handle the various sizes to see which is comfortable for you. Personally, I only use one when working with floppy fabrics to help keep my tension even. I find generally I like to be able to manoeuvre the fabric in my hands without the constraint of the hoop, the natural stiffness of some fabrics being enough to keep tension balanced. So, whether or not to use a frame is very much your choice.

SETTING TO WORK

Before starting fix a short piece of each thread to a strip of card and number it. This will help you identify the shade, invaluable if you find yourself working in a poor light (which should be avoided) or artificial light when tones, particularly of blues, greens and pinks can subtly alter.

With larger projects it is best (time consuming, I know) to protect the edges of the fabric to prevent fraying, which linen, in particular, is prone to do. To do this, either turn under a small hem all round and tack down or bind the edges with masking tape. This is generally unnecessary with small projects.

The starting point on a stitching chart is generally indicated, as is the case for all the projects in these books. For small designs this is usually in the centre, so that it is helpful to be able to find the centre of your fabric quickly. To do this fold the fabric in half lengthwise and crosswise and crease lightly. For larger projects you may find it useful to tack through the centre vertical and horizontal lines created by folding the fabric, so that these provide permanent reference points when stitching the design. On smaller projects just the creased cross should be enough to get you started. Some patterns give the start stitch in one corner or in the middle of one edge of the pattern, so you will not need to do the above tacking or creasing, just follow the instructions as to the start point.

Thread your needle with the directed number of strands. Do not knot the end as this creates lumps which make an uneven surface on the embroidery and knots can unravel. To commence the first stitch, pull the thread through from the reverse side leaving a tail of about 2 inches (5 cm).

◆ **Single cross stitch**

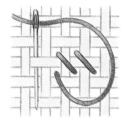

◆ **Cross stitch row**

Hold this tail under the fabric as you work the next stitch. After a few stitches you can either darn the tail in at the back or catch it under with the subsequent stitches. Fasten off by drawing the thread, on the reverse side, through the back of some stitches.

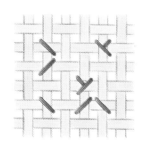

◆ **Half cross stitch**

All the projects in this book use simple cross stitch for most of the design, half cross stitch for some of the shaping and back stitch for outlining. Use the simple half cross stitch for shaping on the edge of a motif and the three quarters version when required in the middle of a design.

If you are a novice, follow the diagrams on a spare piece of fabric to practise.

It is important that the top half of the stitches should all slant in the same direction, otherwise the finished work will look uneven.

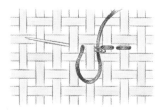

◆ **Backstitch**

All the patterns are worked from colour charts. One square on the chart represents one stitch worked over one or two thread inter-sections on the fabric as directed in the individual instructions. Half squares on the chart denote half cross

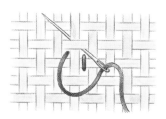

◆ **Angled backstitch**

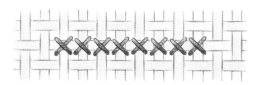

◆ **Over one thread intersection**

◆ **Over two thread intersections**

stitches, the direction of the diagonal indicating the direc-tion of the stitch. If stitches of one shade are scattered close by each other but not immediately abutting each other, it is acceptable to thread the strands through the backs of some of the other stitches to the next point of stitching, but do this only where there is close proximity of stitch, otherwise the overall tension will become distorted.

Using more than one needle

It is useful, when working a design where groups of stitches in the same shade are close to each other, to use more than one needle. When you have stitched the first group, take the needle through to the reverse of the fabric and secure it loosely in a position where it will not interfere with the next stitches you will work. Using the second needle, work the second shade and fasten the needle at the back of the work, as before. Now remove the first needle and thread it through the back of the stitches just worked, so that it is in the right position to work the second group of stitches in the first shade. This can only be done where groups of stitches in the same shade are separated by just three or four squares. If you carry thread over a larger distance, you may produce an uneven tension and on a low count of fabric the lines of thread may show through to the front.

It is also helpful to have several needles threaded with different shades at the start of a complicated project. This saves time once you are stitching.

Estimating fabric size

The finished size of the stitching area is given with each project, so that if you wish to adapt the design you can work out how the dimensions will change.

If you wish to work one of the projects in this book on a different count of fabric from that recommended, you will need to calculate how much fabric to allow, which is very simple. Count the number of squares on the design chart a) down one vertical edge and b) across one horizontal edge. Divide each of these figures by the count of the fabric you wish to use, e.g. by 14 or 16. This will give you the finished design size in inches. Multiply by 2.54 if you wish to have the size in centimetres.

If the work is to be mounted in a frame, add 6 in (15 cm) to each dimension for the fabric size. This allows a good 3 in (7.5 cm) for the framer to use and a 1 in (2.5 cm) hem allowance (to prevent fraying while working).

For fabric size on smaller projects, add 3 in (7.5 cm) to the dimensions of the design, and to fit a particular mount, measure its width and depth, then add on 3 in (7.5 cm).

Letter spacing

This is best worked out on graph paper first, to give a good visual image of how the letters will look. Map out the letters in each horizontal row in pencil on the graph paper, leaving one stitch square between each letter and three between each word. Note that letters which have sloping sides, such as A, W, V, may look better more closely grouped, i.e. without the unstitched square in between.

Now count up the number of horizontal squares in the row and divide by two to find the central point. Where the letters are to be placed centrally on the design, this point will correspond to the centre vertical line of the design. Begin stitching at this point.

For designs where the text is positioned off-centre, refer to the appropriate chart for the starting point. Do map out the letters on graph paper first, though, as you may need to adjust the placing slightly.

FINISHING OFF AND MOUNTING

Tidy your work as you stitch, fastening each thread off by darning it into the back other stitches. Snip off any loose ends.

If the piece needs to be cleaned or freshened up, follow the instructions for washing and pressing given above.

Mounting into card-based mounts, e.g. calendars, greeting cards

Trim the finished piece of work to a slightly smaller size than the mount. Touch fabric adhesive to the edges of the mount and with the design uppermost on a flat surface, place the mount, centrally or as directed, onto the design. At this stage you can pad the design with a little wadding to bring it forward in the mount and soften the edges of the cut-out area. To do this, cut a piece of lightweight wadding just a little larger than the aperture of the mount, touch with glue and fix to the reverse of the embroidered piece. Next glue around the edges of the back of the card or mount backing board and attach it to the back of the embroidery, enclosing the design. Take your time, I have seen too many examples of beautiful stitchwork ruined by bad mounting.

Pots and jars

Back your work with iron-on interfacing before placing in the mount. This has a dual purpose a) it will help prevent fraying and b) it will enable the design to sit more firmly in the mount and not crumple. Iron the interfacing on before you trim the fabric to size. Follow the manufacturers' instructions to assemble the mounts, which are usually simply a matter of trimming the embroidery to fit and placing it in the jar or pot with the backing material in a particular sequence.

Pictures

It is well worth paying for professional mounting. All the effort you have put into the stitching deserves the best!

I like to stretch my work over lightweight wadding as I think it gives a good relief, softening the lines and pushing the stitching forward. A professional framer will lace the work with the wadding over the backing board for you.

A FINAL WORD

Do keep your work in a bag in between stitching: the fabric does tend to pick up dust. But most importantly, after all the rules of 'do's and don'ts', enjoy your craft, be experimental and have fun with creating and stitching the heirlooms of the future!

ACKNOWLEDGEMENTS
The Author and Publishers would
like to thank the following people
for their help in the production of
this book:

For supplying props for
photography: Past Times, Witney,
Oxon, OX8 6BH, UK

For suppying materials for the
projects: DMC Creative World,
Pullman Road, Wigston,
Leicestershire, LE18 2DY, UK

Framecraft Miniatures Ltd,
372-376 Summer Lane, Hockley ,
Birmingham, B19 3QA, UK
(with stockists worldwide)

Impress, Slough Farm, Westhall,
Halesworth, Suffolk IP19 8RN, UK

Kernowcraft Woodturning,
The Courtyard Shopping Mews, 9
High Street, St Ives, Cornwall,
TR26 1RS, UK

For help with the stitching:
Sally Harvey; Annie Jones; Sally
Mason; Barbara Matthews

STOCKISTS
Brooch; clock; crystal pot; desk pen
set; door protector; dressing table set;
lacy bookmark; pre-stretched silk;
Sal-Em products; wooden pot:
Framecraft Miniatures Ltd

Greetings cards; money box; noteblock; notebooks; stationery set:
Impress

Pincushion base: Kernowcraft
Woodturning

Schonfells damask: DMC Creative
World

KITS
All the stitched projects within this
book may be purchased in kit form
(excluding charts) from: Stitchkits, 8
Danescourt Road, Tettenhall,
Wolverhampton, WV6 9BG, UK

PHOTOGRAPH CREDITS
p. 11, p. 86 Sonia Halliday and Laura
Lushington; p. 12, College of Arms ff
105v-106, p. 35 College of Arms Ms
L. 12c, f.7v; p. 14 and p. 57 (Ms
Douce 253), p. 49 (Ms Douce 253),
p. 56 (Ms Douce 267), p. 83 (Ms
Douce 219) Bodleian Library,
Oxford; p. 15, p. 16, p. 19, p. 22,
p. 30, p. 70 Musée de Cluny, ©
R.M.N.; p. 27 Rheinisches Bildarchiv;
p. 40, p. 44, p. 67, p. 68, p. 79
Grammar of Ornament, Studio
Editions, 1986; p. 47, p. 65 British
Library; p. 59 European Art in the
14th Century, Artia, 1978; p. 60 E T
Archive/Victoria & Albert Museum;
p. 62, p. 78 The Board of Trustees,
Victoria and Albert Museum; p. 74
Hessisches Landesmuseum,
Darmstadt; p. 77 Historisches
Museum, Basel: Maurice Babey; p. 81
Michael Holford